QA
76.9
.D3
J32
1988

RELATIONAL DATABASE DESIGN WITH MICROCOMPUTER APPLICATIONS

GLENN A. JACKSON

Oakland University

Prentice Hall
Englewood Cliffs, New Jersey 07632

Library of Congress Cataloging-in-Publication Data

Jackson, Glenn A.
    Relational database design with microcomputer
applications.

    Bibliography.
    Includes index.
    1. Relational data bases.   2. Microcomputers—
Programming.   I. Title.
QA76.9.D3J32   1988   005.75´6   87-14462
ISBN 0-13-771841-1

Editorial/production supervision
and interior design: Carolyn Fellows
Cover design: Wanda Lubelska Design
Manufacturing buyer: Gordon Osbourne

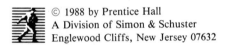 © 1988 by Prentice Hall
A Division of Simon & Schuster
Englewood Cliffs, New Jersey 07632

Printed in the United States of America

10 9 8 7 6 5 4 3 2

ISBN 0-13-771841-1   025

PRENTICE-HALL INTERNATIONAL (UK) LIMITED, *London*
PRENTICE-HALL OF AUSTRALIA PTY. LIMITED, *Sydney*
PRENTICE-HALL CANADA INC., *Toronto*
PRENTICE-HALL HISPANOAMERICANA, S.A., *Mexico*
PRENTICE-HALL OF INDIA PRIVATE LIMITED, *New Delhi*
PRENTICE-HALL OF JAPAN, INC., *Tokyo*
SIMON & SCHUSTER ASIA PTE. LTD., *Singapore*
EDITORA PRENTICE-HALL DO BRASIL, LTDA., *Rio de Janeiro*

Dedicated to my wife
MAY
and to our two sons
ALAN and MARK

CONTENTS

PREFACE

As the title indicates, this book is an introduction to relational database design. It is not intended to be an introduction to the use of a particular database management system, or a general introduction to a specific query language. Although it is true that a reader who studies the topics in this text will become well acquainted with dBASE II/III® and R:base 5000®, the main emphasis of the book is the investigation of the problem of designing the database to be used with a standard database management system, like dBASE III[1]. The goal is to outline a database design process that can be understood by an average microcomputer user. This user may have purchased a relational database system like dBASE II, dBASE III, R:base 5000 or some similar package, and has come to the startling conclusion that before a database can be implemented, the structure of the database must be designed.

The documentation that accompanies most database management system (DBMS) packages that are purchased "off-the-shelf" from a software vendor, assumes that the buyer has a ready-made database in need of a DBMS. In fact, the buyer usually has a large data storage problem that looks as though it could be solved by using a DBMS. The buyer normally doesn't know how to design the database, and finds that the user's manual

---

[1] dBASE II and dBASE III are registered trademarks of Ashton-Tate. R:base 5000 is a registered trademark of Microrim, Inc.

is of little help. Since the success or failure of the overall system will depend upon an intelligent design procedure, it is important that the user realizes that systematic design procedures are available. It is the purpose of this text to outline some of these procedures.

To the beginner, a relational database is visualized as a set of tables, or files (really relations, as we shall see). If these tables are not designed correctly, data in the database may be erroneously changed, or deleted, when the DBMS is used. Typical problems that can arise are

1. The user wishes to delete information related to the shipments from a certain supplier. The command to delete these data ends up deleting the name and address of the supplier, in addition to the shipment data.
2. The user tries to correct the spelling of the name of a given client. However, the user forgets that the name is stored in three different places. The end result is that only one of the three names gets changed, and the true spelling of the name of the client is now in doubt.

These are just two simple examples of the type of problems that can arise if the relations in the database are not properly designed. Conversely, they are exactly the types of problems that will be eliminated if the relations are designed correctly.

The theory of relational database design is based on the mathematical theory of relations. Indeed, one prime reason for the wide acceptance of the relational database approach is that mathematical theory has been used to develop algorithmic methods of design. Since most users of microcomputer-based database systems are not professional mathematicians, it would seem that they would benefit from a text that detailed sound design principles, but tried to minimize mathematical formalism. This is one goal of this text: some mathematical formalism is contained in the text, since it is nearly impossible to discuss relations without it; however, the level of the mathematics has been held to a minimum, and presented in a form that can be understood by a general population of readers.

The book is divided into four logical parts. Part one (Chapters 1 and 2) deals with the definition and properties of relations, the definition of a relational database, and examples of the problems that arise when a database is poorly designed. Part two (Chapters 3, 4, and 5) deals with the concept of functional dependencies and how they are used with design algorithms to develop a final database. This section includes an in-depth study of a typical database design problem. Part three (Chapters 6, 7, and 8) introduces a second design method using entity-relationship models. Part four gives complete implementations of the case study database in both dBASE III (Chapter 9) and R:base 5000 (Chapter 10). This section of the book illustrates the fact that some database queries will require the use of a high level language, rather than a simple application of database commands. Sample dBASE II and dBASE III queries are used throughout the text to emphasize certain aspects of the theory being presented.

The text assumes that the reader has a good high school background in mathematics, and that he or she can think through a problem in a logical manner. The material presented should be of value to any beginning database designer, and to the managers who supervise those designers. The text should serve as an ideal reference in a beginning course in database management systems for business and management majors. The length of the text has been held to a minimum in the hope that this will encourage readers to read it completely.

ACKNOWLEDGMENTS

Many Oakland University students have read various portions of the manuscript for this book. Their comments and constructive criticisms are very much appreciated. Two students deserve particular mention: Ms. Judith Ireland, who developed the original version of the Bowling Secretary's Database found in Chapter 5; and Ms. Barbara MacNeil, who developed the basic logic and dBASE III implementation for the team standings program module found in Chapter 9.

DISCLAIMER

The names of persons and organizations used in the examples, problems, and case studies in this book are purposely fictitious. Any names that are the same as those of actual people or organizations are strictly coincidental.

1

DATABASES, RELATIONS, AND RELATIONAL DATABASES

1.1 BASIC CONCEPTS

A **database** may be defined as a unified collection of data that is to be shared by all authorized personnel in an enterprise. The enterprise could be a company, a department in a company, a bank, or a school. The purpose of the database is to store all of the data of interest to the enterprise in one location, so that redundant data storage within the enterprise is eliminated. When multiple copies of data are stored at different locations within an enterprise, discrepancies will arise between supposedly identical sets of data. At this point it may be impossible to determine which of two differing sets of data is correct. In a well-designed database, redundant data are eliminated and the probability of storing inconsistent data is minimized.

On large mainframe computer systems, the data in a database can be accessed concurrently by over a hundred users. The database in such cases may have hundreds of fields of data with millions of pieces of information. Such a system could hold literally every piece of data required to operate the enterprise. Databases on microcomputer systems are on a more modest scale. Here, a single database is usually accessed by only one user at a time, and each database holds only a subset of the data for the enterprise. One database might be developed to hold financial information, while a second database would be developed to hold personnel data.

Whether the database being developed is to be stored in a mainframe, or in a micro, the function of the **database management system** (DBMS) is the same. The DBMS is the software-hardware package that makes the database easily accessible to the users. As seen in Figure 1.1, a software portion of the DBMS that some manufacturers call the database manager serves as an interface between the user and the database. The database manager provides the software tools required to create, load, query, and update data in the database. The database manager also handles all I/O and memory management related to the database, and on larger systems it handles security and concurrent user problems. In short, a well-designed DBMS will provide software which makes it easy for a user to communicate with the database.

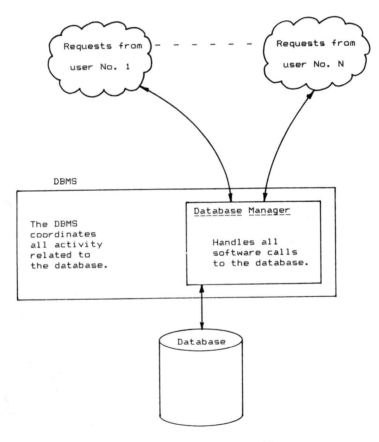

Figure 1.1 Overview of a DBMS architecture.

Another similarity between large and small database management systems is that in both cases the database itself must be well designed if the database system, as a whole, is to perform properly. The purpose of this text is to outline some basic design procedures for one particular type of database structure, namely a relational database. The examples in this text assume that the user will implement the database on a microcomputer system; however, the same design algorithms apply to databases being designed for larger computer systems.

1.2 DEFINITION OF A RELATION

Mathematically, a relation is defined as follows:

> Given "N" sets, D1,D2, ...,DN, R is a **relation** over these sets, if R is a set of ordered n-tuples of the form ⟨d1,d2, ...,dn⟩ where d1 is an element from D1, d2 is an element from D2, ..., and dn is an element from DN. D1,D2, ...,DN are called the **domains** of R.

The meaning of this definition is most easily described by a graphical representation, as in Figure 1.2. Here there are four domains. Domain D1 is a set of integers; D2 is a set of character strings that are names of things; D3 is a set of character strings that are colors; and D4 is another set of integers. The relation shown has six tuples. Each **tuple** consists of four elements where each element has been picked from a different domain. Note that the order of the elements in the tuples is important; the first element in every tuple is from domain D1, the second element in every tuple is from D2, etc.

A "data processing view" of a relation is given in Figure 1.3. Here it is seen that the four domains given in Figure 1.2 have been related to four real world items: part number, part name, part color, and part weight. The relation now looks like a table, or a file, and the tuples look like rows of a table, or records in a file. The names of the columns, which a data processing-type would call fields in a record, are termed **attributes,** and the individual values that appear in a given tuple are called **attribute values.** Thus, the first element in the first tuple has an attribute value of 101, and was taken from a domain of pnum's. In this text, the following sets of terms will be used more or less interchangeably:

1. relation, table, and file.
2. tuple, row, and record.
3. attribute, column, and field.

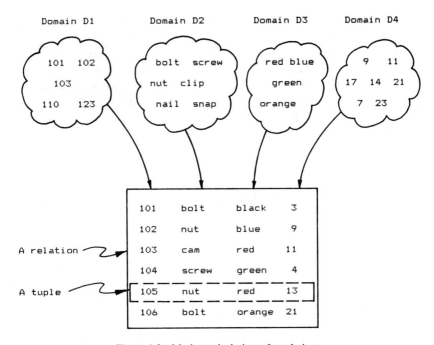

Figure 1.2   Mathematical view of a relation.

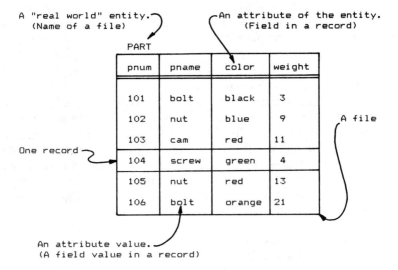

Figure 1.3   Data processing view of a relation.

This is not being done because it is mathematically correct (Which it isn't!), but because most microcomputer database system documentation uses the terms given interchangeably.

One comment on the difference between the mathematical definition of a relation and the actual storage of relations in microcomputer database systems is worth noting. By definition, a relation can have no two tuples that are identical. Although most large DBMS's won't allow the storage of identical tuples (records) in a relation (file), many microcomputer DBMS's will allow it, unless special programming techniques are used to avoid it.

There are two additional terms concerning relations that should be mentioned. The number of columns in a relation is called the **degree** of the relation. The number of tuples that are currently in a relation is the **cardinality** of the relation. The degree of a relation normally doesn't change after creation, but the cardinality will fluctuate as new tuples are added or old tuples are deleted.

1.3 DEFINITION OF A RELATIONAL DATABASE

A **relational database** is nothing more than a collection of relations that contains all the information that is to be stored in the database. Figure 1.4 is an example of a very small relational database called the Supplier_Parts database. This database holds three types of information about a construction company[1]:

1. Information on suppliers who supply parts to the enterprise. This includes supplier numbers, which are assumed to be unique, and supplier names, status and home city, none of which are unique. This is the Sup relation.
2. Information on parts that are used by the enterprise. This includes part numbers, which are unique, and part names, colors, and weight, none of which are unique. This is the Part relation.
3. Information on the part numbers and quantities of each part that is currently being supplied by each supplier. This is the SP relation.

Each relation in the database is stored as an individual file. The structure of the file used to store a relation is fairly simple, since every record in the file has exactly the same format. On larger DBMS's each relation is

---

[1]The Supplier_Parts database appears frequently in database literature. It is a good example of a small relational database. The creator of this database does not appear to be credited by any of the authors who use it.

PART

pnum	pname	color	weight
101	bolt	black	3
102	nut	blue	9
103	cam	red	11
104	screw	green	4
105	nut	red	13
106	bolt	orange	21

SUP

snum	sname	status	city
S1	Smith	20	London
S2	Jones	15	Detroit
S3	Adder	10	Chicago
S4	House	30	Paris
S5	Blake	20	Paris

SP

snum	pnum	qty
S1	101	9
S1	102	4
S1	103	2
S1	106	3
S2	101	3
S2	102	8
S2	105	11
S2	106	9
S3	101	7
S3	102	13
S3	103	6
S3	104	1
S3	105	2
S3	106	5
S4	103	7
S4	106	13
S5	103	8
S5	104	9

Figure 1.4   The Supplier_Parts database.

stored as an indexed file, where the index is an attribute, or set of attributes, that is specified by the creator of the relation. The set of attributes used for the index is called the primary key of the relation. The **primary key** is defined as that attribute, or set of attributes, which can be used to identify uniquely one tuple in a relation from another. A primary key must not have any extra attributes. This means that if any one attribute is dropped from the primary key, the remaining attributes are not sufficient to identify one tuple uniquely from another. In the Supplier_Parts database, the primary keys are ⟨snum⟩ for the Sup relation, ⟨pnum⟩ for the Part relation, and the pair of attributes ⟨snum,pnum⟩ for the SP relation.

Readers should satisfy themselves that each primary key is sufficient to identify each tuple uniquely in a relation. For instance, in the SP relation, if snum = 'S1' and pnum = 101, there should be no more than one tuple that can be found that has these particular attribute values. In Figure 1.4, the tuple with these values is ⟨S1, 101, 9⟩. If another tuple, with the same primary key, say ⟨S1, 101, 11⟩, were to be stored in the relation, confusion would result, since it would not be known whether S1 was supplying 9, or 11, of part 101 (or maybe 20?). In a fully developed relational DBMS, an error message will be generated when a user tries to store a tuple that has a primary key equal to one already in the relation. In many microcomputer-based DBMS implementations, tuples with identical primary keys, and even tuples that are identical, can be stored in a relation without a DBMS error occurring. This is unfortunate and can lead to some problems, as will be shown later in the book.

In many DBMS's, an index on a file containing a relation is not created automatically, and the user must execute an INDEX command to create an index. Indexing a file speeds up execution of some commands rather dramatically. It is possible to have an index into a relation using an attribute other than the primary key. This type of index file is called a **secondary index** and is, again, used to reduce access time when locating data in the relation. A simplified example of an index file is given in Figure 1.5. Note that the relation itself is normally not sorted into any particular order, and can have missing rows where tuples have been deleted, but the index file is sorted. Index files can have many different structures, and are usually developed in some sort of tree structure so that they can be searched quickly. The structure of the index file in Figure 1.5 was chosen for illustration purposes, and is not intended to imply that it is a practical design.

The number of relations that end up in a database and the specific attributes that are assigned to each relation are determined by the design process. The design process itself may be quite lengthy. However, once the design has been completed, the creation of the database within the DBMS can be accomplished rather quickly. In the case of the Supplier_Parts database, the database structure is completely specified by the short set of statements given in Figure 1.6. This short description of the database is called the **conceptual model** of the database and holds all of the information necessary to create the complete database structure, regardless of which DBMS is being used. Figure 1.7 is an example of how the Sup relation is created in dBASE II, along with an index file for Sup where the index is over the primary key. Each relation in the Supplier_Parts database would be created in a similar manner. Note that all the information needed to create Sup is contained in the conceptual model. After a relation has been created, it is said to be **unpopulated,** and must be loaded a tuple-at-a-time using appropriate store commands.

A listing of the contents of a relation, or of all the relations in a database, such as the one of the Supplier_Parts database given in Figure 1.4, should be thought of as a snapshot of what the relations could look like at

Supx (Index File)   Sup (Data File)

Record No.	snum	Sup File Record No.		Record No.	snum	sname	status	city
0001	S1	0006		0001	S4	House	30	Paris
0002	S2	0004		0002	S5	Blake	20	Paris
0003	S3	0003		0003	S3	Adder	10	Chicago
0004	S4	0001		0004	S2	Jones	15	Detroit
0005	S5	0002		0005	This record has been deleted			
				0006	S1	Smith	20	London

Figure 1.5 Simple example of an index file.

```
Database Name: Supplier_Parts.
Attributes and type:
    snum      char(3),
    sname     char(6),
    status    integer,
    city      char(10),
    pnum      integer,
    pname     char(6),
    color     char(6),
    weight    integer,
    qty       integer.
Relations and <Primary Keys>:
    Sup(snum, sname, status, city)  <snum>,
    SP(snum, pnum, qty)  <snum, pnum>,
    Part(pnum, pname, color, weight)  <pnum>.
```

Figure 1.6   Conceptual model of the Supplier_Parts database.

```
. CREATE
ENTER FILENAME: B:Sup
ENTER RECORD STRUCTURE AS FOLLOWS:
    FIELD    NAME,TYPE,WIDTH,DECIMAL PLACES
    001      snum,c,3
    002      sname,c,6
    003      status,n,2
    004      city,c,10
    005
INPUT DATA NOW? N
. USE B:Sup
. INDEX ON snum TO B:Supx
.
```

Figure 1.7   Creating a relation and an index file for that relation in dBASE II.

some instant in time. It should be remembered that the contents of all relations are dynamic, since tuples can be added, deleted, or modified during
the lifetime of a relation. The particular listing of any relation at some
instant in time is called an **instance** of that relation.

The primary key defined for a relation is so significant that the attributes, or set of attributes, that form the primary key are usually noted
when the mathematical form of the relation is written down. In this text
the attributes that form the primary key will be noted by having them
underlined. As an example, the SP relation defined in Figure 1.6 will be
written as SP(snum, pnum, qty), indicating that the pair of attributes
⟨snum,pnum⟩ is the primary key for this relation.

2

THE NEED
FOR DATABASE DESIGN

2.1 DESIGN GOALS

Before looking at specific design problems and algorithms, it is best to outline some design goals. In particular, what is the desired end result of the
relational database design process? Although many design goals can be set,
the following goals are considered to be the most important ones:

1. Have the capability of storing all pertinent data in the database;
2. Eliminate redundant data;
3. Keep the number of relations in the database to a minimum;
4. Have the relations normalized, so as to minimize update and deletion
   problems.

Each of these goals will be discussed briefly.

   Goal 1: Capability of storing all pertinent data in the database.
This goal is rather obvious, but still very important. The database is sup-
posed to hold all data of interest to the enterprise, so the database must be

designed in such a manner that a place for all pertinent data can be found in the database. The first step in the design process is the determination of all of the attributes that are to be placed in the database. Once the attributes have been identified, the designer can begin to worry about how many relations will be needed, and which attributes will go into which relation. In a microcomputer-based database, there is the additional problem of deciding whether the data to be stored should be conceptualized as being in only one database, or possibly two or more databases.

Goal 2: Eliminate redundant data.   The ramifications of this goal are not at all obvious to the beginning database designer. The key to understanding this goal is to realize that there is a distinct difference between **duplicated data** and **redundantly duplicated data.** As an example, look at the E_S relation in Figure 2.1(a). This relation has two attributes, Emp# (employee number) and Supr (supervisor). The relation holds data that indicates the immediate supervisor of each employee in the enterprise. The names of supervisors can show up several times in the relation. In fact, a supervisor's name will appear once for each employee supervised. Note, however, that although 'Jones' and 'Smith' both appear twice in the instance of E_S given in Figure 2.1(a), neither of the duplicated names is redundant. The reason they are not redundant is that if one of the names is dropped from the relation, information is lost. For example, Figure 2.1(b) shows what an instance of E_S would look like with the duplicated names deleted. In this case, there is no way of knowing the names of the supervisors for employees #195 and #200.

Figure 2.2(a) is an example of a relation that does have redundantly duplicated data. Relation E_S_P is similar to the relation E_S, but in-

E_S

Emp#	Supr
125	Jones
138	Smith
195	Smith
200	Jones

(a)

E_S

Emp#	Supr
125	Jones
138	Smith
195	—
200	—

(b)

Figure 2.1 Duplicate data that is not redundant.

E_S_P

Emp#	Supr	Sphone
125	Jones	3051
135	Smith	2222
195	Smith	2222
200	Jones	3051

(a)

E_S_P

Emp#	Supr	Sphone
125	Jones	3051
135	Smith	2222
195	Smith	–
200	Jones	–

(b)

E_S

Emp#	Supr
125	Jones
138	Smith
195	Smith
200	Jones

S_P

Supr	Sphone
Jones	3051
Smith	2222

(c)

Figure 2.2   Eliminating redundant data.

cludes the attribute Sphone, which is the phone number of the supervisor. (It is assumed that each supervisor has only one phone number.) In this instance the phone numbers for Jones and Smith appear more than once, and the duplicated information on phone numbers is redundant. The reason the duplicate phone numbers are redundant is that if, say, one of the phone numbers for Jones is eliminated, Jones' phone number is still available in other tuples in the relation. Figure 2.2(b) is an example of how the E_S_P relation would look if the duplicate phone numbers were replaced with 'nulls'. Note that the phone numbers for Jones and Smith have not been lost, since they each appear in one tuple in the relation. This method of handling redundant data is not satisfactory for two reasons. First, null fields in a database should be avoided, since extra programming is required to figure out what the null really means. In this case, if the third tuple, ⟨195, Smith, − ⟩, were read from the relation, the phone number of Smith would not be known. The user would have to know enough to look up another tuple in the relation that had Smith as the Supr attribute value and a non-null value for Sphone. Second, and more critically, the relation in Figure 2.2(b) is structured so that severe deletion problems can occur. If the employee with E# = 125 leaves the enterprise, and the tuple ⟨125, Jones, 3051⟩ is deleted from the relation to take this fact into account, the phone number for Jones is lost, since it doesn't appear anywhere else in the relation.

Figure 2.2(c) shows a better way of eliminating the redundant phone numbers. Here the E_S_P relation has been replaced by two relations, one holding information on employee numbers and supervisor names, and one holding information on supervisor phone numbers. It will be shown in the next chapter that splitting relations is a standard design procedure, but must be done under certain constraints. Note in Figure 2.2(c) that employee #125 can now be deleted from the E _ S relation without losing the phone number of the employee's former supervisor, which is stored in the S _ P relation.

Goal 3: Keep the number of relations to a minimum. This goal deals with the fact that although splitting one relation into two or more smaller relations may be desirable for the elimination of certain problems, too many relations in the database may make it cumbersome to use from a user's standpoint. Thus, the number of relations can't be allowed to grow in an unlimited manner.

Goal 4: Have the relations normalized. Goal four deals with the fact that certain relations are more susceptible to deletion and update problems, such as the loss of the supervisor's phone number discussed in goal two above, than are other relations. The designer must learn to spot these potentially dangerous relations and "normalize them" by splitting them in a prescribed manner. **Normalization** is the decomposition of one relation into two or more relations following a specific procedure to determine the split. Normalization will be discussed in Chapter 3.

One problem with design goals three and four is that they work in opposition to each other. Goal three may have to be compromised to meet goal four or, conversely, goal four may have to be compromised to meet goal three. This will be part of the final design decision.

2.2 THE UNIVERSAL RELATION

Assume that a small database is to be designed for a college advisor. The advisor has many student advisees, all of whom live on campus, and all of whom are in the same major department.

The first step in the design process is the determination of all the attributes that the advisor wishes to have in the database, and how the attributes are related to each other. This information is obtained through in-depth discussions with the advisor, making certain that the advisor knows what data are to be in the database, how the database will be used, and what information the advisor expects to get from the database. After several sessions with the advisor, the names and conditions on the attributes to be stored were determined to be:

Snum- Student number. An integer that has a unique value for each student in the university.

Sname- Student name. Each student has only one name, but it is possible that more than one student has the same name.

Rnum- Campus dormitory room number. Every student lives on campus and is assigned a room. More than one student may be assigned to a single room.

Pnum- Student phone number. Each campus dormitory room has one phone that is shared by all the students in that room.

Class- Class number. This is the identification number of a class taken by a particular student. An example would be MTH122. The advisor will only store data on classes that have been completed by a given student.

Term- College term. This is the college term in which a given class was completed by the student. It is possible that a given student may take the same course over in different terms.

Grade- Class grade. The grade that a given student received in a particular class in a given term.

A sample of the data that the advisor conceptualizes as being stored in the database is shown in Figure 2.3. Although this figure is a tabular example of the data that might be in the database at some instant in time, the table is not a relation.

To illustrate why the table in Figure 2.3 is not a relation, one "row" of the table has been pulled out in Figure 2.4. In this figure, the field values in the four fields Snum, Sname, Rnum, and Pnum are all single-valued, while the values in the fields of Class, Term, and Grade have multiple values. This "row" is obviously different from the shape of the tuples that were given in the simple relations discussed earlier. The difference is that

ADVISOR

Snum	Sname	Rnum	Pnum	Class	Term	Grade
3215	JonesG	120DH	2136	MTH122	F84	1.6
				SCI120	F84	2.4
				PHY230	W85	2.1
				MTH122	W85	2.3
3462	SmithA	238VH	2344	MTH122	W84	2.3
				MTH123	W85	3.5
				PSY220	W85	3.7
3567	HowesJ	120DH	2136	SCI239	W84	3.3
				EGR171	F84	3.5
				PHY141	F84	1.8
4756	AlexK	345VH	3321	MUS389	F83	4.0

Figure 2.3 Data desired by the advisor.

3215	JonesG	120DH	2136	MTH122	F84	1.6
				SCI120	F84	2.4
				PHY230	W85	2.1
				MTH122	W85	2.3

Figure 2.4   One "row" from the table in Figure 2.3.

all of the fields in the row do not contain single-valued attributes. To force the data in Figure 2.3 into the form of a relation, the data must be rearranged so that every tuple has a single-valued item in each element of the tuple. This can usually be done by a simple insertion process, with the result in this case being Figure 2.5. This process forces the addition of a large amount of redundant data, but the redundancy will be removed later in the design process.

The table in Figure 2.5 is now an instance of a legitimate relation. It is referred to as the **universal relation** for the database being designed. The universal relation has all the attributes of interest placed into one relation, and could store all the data that is to be placed in the database at a future time. For small databases (ones with no more than 15–20 attributes) the universal relation can be used effectively as the starting point for database design.

2.3 PROBLEMS WITH USING A SINGLE RELATION

A beginning designer would be tempted to use the ADVISOR relation in Figure 2.5 as the complete database. It appears to be the straightforward thing to do. Why break ADVISOR into several smaller relations, when it

ADVISOR

Snum	Sname	Rnum	Pnum	Class	Term	Grade
3215	JonesG	120DH	2136	MTH122	F84	1.6
3215	JonesG	120DH	2136	SCI120	F84	2.4
3215	JonesG	120DH	2136	PHY230	W85	2.1
3215	JonesG	120DH	2136	MTH122	W85	2.3
3462	SmithA	238VH	2344	MTH122	W84	2.3
3462	SmithA	238VH	2344	MTH123	W85	3.5
3462	SmithA	238VH	2344	PSY220	W85	3.7
3567	HowesJ	120DH	2136	SCI239	W84	3.3
3567	HowesJ	120DH	2136	EGR171	F84	3.5
3567	HowesJ	120DH	2136	PHY141	F84	1.8
4756	AlexK	345VH	3321	MUS389	F83	4.0

Figure 2.5   The data from the table in Figure 2.3 placed in a legal relation.

can hold all of the data by itself? There are several reasons why this particular relation should not be used as the only one in the database. This can be discovered by visualizing how the database will be used, and how the data in ADVISOR will be affected by certain database operations. The discussion below centers on three specific problems: one related to update (or modification) of data in the database; one involving deletion of a tuple; and another involving insertion of a new tuple. The problems outlined are generally referred to as insertion, deletion, and update anomalies, where an anomaly is a variation from the norm.

Insertion problem: If the advisor is assigned a new advisee, one who has not yet completed a class, a tuple for that student would have to be placed in the database with nulls for Class, Term, and Grade attribute values. As has been noted several times, null values should be avoided. Thus, the new student couldn't be added to the database until after a class had been completed.

Figure 2.6(a) is an example of what ADVISOR would look like if a student who hadn't completed any classes was forced into the relation using dBASE II. The null character strings show up as blank fields (in Class and Term), while the null numeric value in the Grade field is interpreted by dBASE II as a 0.0. Figure 2.6(b) shows a possible consequence of the 0.0 appearing in place of the null. Here a solution to the query "List the Snums

```
use advisor
. list
00001    3215 JonesG    120DH    2136 MTH122 F84    1.6
00002    3215 JonesG    120DH    2136 SCI120 F84    2.4
00003    3215 JonesG    120DH    2136 PHY230 W85    2.1
00004    3215 JonesG    120DH    2136 MTH122 W85    2.3
00005    3462 SmithA    238VH    2344 MTH122 W84    2.3
00006    3462 SmithA    238VH    2344 MTH123 W85    3.5
00007    3462 SmithA    238VH    2344 PSY220 W85    3.7
00008    3567 HowesJ    120DH    2136 SCI239 W84    3.3
00009    3567 HowesJ    120DH    2136 EGR171 F84    3.5
00010    3567 HowesJ    120DH    2136 PHY141 F84    1.8
00011    4756 AlexK     345VH    3321 MUS389 F83    4.0
00012    7890 HomerH    121VH    7619               0.0
```

(a)

```
. display off Snum, Sname for Grade < 2.0
  3215 JonesG
  3567 HowesJ
  7890 HomerH
  .
```

(b)

Figure 2.6   (a) Result of inserting a record with null fields; (b) query error due to null fields.

and Snames of all students who have received at least one grade below a 2.0'' has been executed. HomerH is listed as such a student, but HomerH hasn't completed a single class!

Update problem: There is a large amount of redundant data in AD-VISOR. Redundant data always signals the possibility of modifying only part of the desired data during an update operation. ADVISOR has both obvious, and not-so-obvious, redundancy. The obvious redundancy is that a given student's name, room number and phone number may be listed several times. In the instance of ADVISOR given in Figure 2.5, Ms. G. Jones' room number appears three times. If she calls her advisor and says that her room number has been changed, the advisor must make certain that this change is made in all three tuples, or the data will be inconsistent.

A not-so-obvious redundancy is that the same phone number shows up for all students who live in the same room. In Figure 2.5 the phone number for room 120DH appears both with JonesG and HowesJ. Assume Ms. G. Jones tells her advisor that her phone number has been changed to 7777, but neglects to tell the advisor that she has a roommate. If the advisor only changes the phone numbers in those tuples that have JonesG's student number in them, then the true phone number for the phone that is in room number 120DH will not be known, since two different numbers for the phone in this room would be in the relation.

Figure 2.7 illustrates the last update anomaly. In Figure 2.7(a), the phone number of JonesG is changed to 7777. Figure 2.7(b) gives the dBASE II answer to the query "List the phone number for the phone in room 120DH." Two numbers are listed in answer to the query, which is in error since each room has only one phone and one phone number. Note that duplicate answers to the query were printed out by dBASE II. The phone numbers 2136 and 7777 each appear in three different tuples in the instance of the ADVISOR relation under discussion, and all six values got printed out by the DBMS. Some DBMS's are programmed to suppress duplicate answers to queries, unless they are specifically requested.

Deletion problems: In the instance of ADVISOR given in Figure 2.5, a tuple with Snum = 4756 appears only once in the relation. This tuple is for a student whose name is AlexK. Assume that the advisor discovers that this student didn't take class MUS389 as indicated, and deletes this tuple from the relation. Since this is the only tuple that contains any information related to this student, its deletion will eliminate this student from the database. If the advisor followed this deletion with a request for a listing of the names of all advisees from ADVISOR, the name of AlexK would not be listed!

```
. list off
3215 JonesG   120DH   2136 MTH122 F84   1.6
3215 JonesG   120DH   2136 SCI120 F84   2.4
3215 JonesG   120DH   2136 PHY230 W85   2.1
3215 JonesG   120DH   2136 MTH122 W85   2.3
3462 SmithA   238VH   2344 MTH122 W84   2.3
3462 SmithA   238VH   2344 MTH123 W85   3.5
3462 SmithA   238VH   2344 PSY220 W85   3.7
3567 HowesJ   120DH   2136 SCI239 W84   3.3
3567 HowesJ   120DH   2136 EGR171 F84   3.5
3567 HowesJ   120DH   2136 PHY141 F84   1.8
4756 AlexK    345VH   3321 MUS389 F83   4.0
7890 HomerH   121VH   7619              0.0
. replace Pnum with 7777 for Sname = 'JonesG'
00004 REPLACEMENT(S)
.
```

(a)

```
. display off Pnum for Rnum = '120DH'
7777
7777
7777
7777
2136
2136
2136
.
```

(b)

Figure 2.7 (a) Changing one student's phone number; (b) query error following the change in phone number.

2.4 PROBLEMS FOR CHAPTER 2

1. What is the primary key for the ADVISOR relation in Figure 2.5?
2. Identify specific examples of data in the ADVISOR relation in Figure 2.5 that are both duplicate and redundant.
3. Identify specific examples of data in the ADVISOR relation in Figure 2.5 that are duplicate, but not redundant.
4. A PHONE relation has been developed to hold information on employee names, home phone numbers, and work phone extension numbers. It is assumed that each employee has a unique name, will list only one home phone number, and may list several work extension numbers. Several employees may share the same phone number. A typical instance of the PHONE relation is given in Figure 2.8.
   a) Discuss which data in the instance of the PHONE relation are redundant.
   b) How should PHONE be changed to eliminate redundant data?

c) Draw instances of the relations you propose to use to eliminate re-dundancy. Include the same data given in Figure 2.8.

PHONE

Name	Hphone	Bus_ext
JonesKK	345-1121	3167
JonesKK	345-1121	3168
KroftAD	345-9898	4000
MartzLK	348-4512	3167
MartzLK	348-4512	3168
RalstonTT	345-7766	4001
RalstonTT	345-7766	4002

Figure 2.8 An instance of the PHONE relation.

3

FUNCTIONAL
DEPENDENCIES

3.1 FIRST NORMAL FORM (1NF)

In Chapter 2, it was stated that relational database design involves the process of splitting relations that exhibit poor properties (from an anomaly standpoint) into new relations that exhibit good properties. Several questions need to be raised regarding this process:

1. Where do you get the relation, or relations, to start the process?
2. How do you know which relations need splitting?
3. How do you go about splitting a relation?
4. How do you know when you are finished?

The answers to these questions will be developed in this chapter and further clarified in Chapter 4.

For databases with fewer than about twenty attributes, the starting point for the process can be visualized as the universal relation. This relation contains all the attributes of interest, and is structured so that each tuple in the relation has single-valued elements. This means that all instances of the relation must have the form shown in Figure 2.5, rather than something like that in Figure 2.3.

Any relation that is in a form such that each element is, and always will be, single-valued is said to be in **first normal form,** or 1NF. A relation must be in first normal form before it can even be considered for reduction into two or more relations.

3.2 CONCEPT OF FUNCTIONAL DEPENDENCIES

The process of splitting a relation to reduce the probability that anomalies will occur is termed **decomposition.** The key to going about decomposition in a logical, methodical way is the concept of functional dependencies between the attributes in the relation under consideration.

A **functional dependency** (FD) is defined as follows:

> Given two attributes, A and B, B is said to be functionally dependent upon A, if every value of A has exactly one value of B associated with it (at any instant of time). A and B may be composite; that is, they may be groups of two or more attributes, rather than a single attribute.

From a practical viewpoint, what this definition says is that if B is functionally dependent upon A, then every tuple that has the same value of A in it must have exactly the same value of B in those same tuples. The values of A and B may change in time, but if they do, they must change in such a way that each unique value of A has only one value of B associated with it. Functional dependencies (FD's) are described using several different kinds of notation. Two of the more common ways are shown in Figure 3.1.

In a real-world situation, functional dependencies are determined by detailing the properties of all the attributes in a relation, and deducing how the attributes relate to one another. Functional dependencies cannot be proven by merely looking at a particular instance of a relation and noting if the same values for two attributes show up in more than one tuple. This may give you a clue as to where to check for FD's, but it is not a proof.

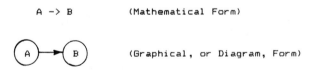

Figure 3.1   Two ways of indicating that attribute B is functionally dependent upon attribute A.

FD's must be deduced from the basic properties of the attributes themselves.

As an example, look at the attributes in the ADVISOR relation in Figure 2.5, and in particular the detailed explanation of how these attributes are related, as detailed in Section 2.2. After reviewing the descriptions of the attributes, the dependencies given in Figure 3.2 can be deduced. The reasoning that led to these FD's will be discussed in detail below:

1. Student numbers are unique. Every student has a Snum, and each student has a different one. Thus, if you know a student's Snum, you know that only one Sname can be associated with it: Snum − ⟩ Sname. The reverse is not true. Sname − ⟩ Snum is not a valid FD, since several students could have exactly the same name.

2. Each student is assigned to one dorm room, but a dorm room may hold more than one student. Thus, Snum − ⟩ Rnum is true but Rnum − ⟩ Snum is not.

3. Since each room has only one phone, and since each phone has a unique phone number, Rnum − ⟩ Pnum and Pnum − ⟩ Rnum. This situation is usually noted as Snum ⟨ − ⟩ Pnum, and Snum and Pnum are said to be **mutually dependent.**

```
Snum   ->   Sname

Snum   ->   Rnum

Rnum   ->   Pnum

Pnum   ->   Rnum

Snum   ->   Pnum

Snum, Class, Term -> Grade
```
(a)

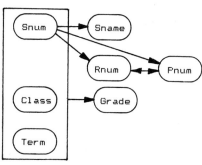

(b)

Figure 3.2 Different notations for the FD's between the attributes in AD-VISOR.

4. Since there is only one phone in a room, and since that phone has a unique number, it follows that only one phone number can be associated with a given student, or Snum $-\rangle$ Pnum.

5. The last FD is an example of a composite set of attributes being involved in the FD. Snum, Class, Term $-\rangle$ Grade says that a grade can be uniquely determined only if you know the Snum of the student who took a given Class in a given Term. (It must be remembered that a student can repeat a class and might get a different grade the second time.)

The reader should check the ADVISOR relation (Figure 2.5) and make certain that the data in that relation checks with the FD's in Figure 3.2. For instance, note that Rnum = 120DH and Pnum = 2136 are always paired together (Rnum $\langle --\rangle$ Pnum); also, Snum = 3215 has only one name associated with it, namely 'JonesG', which it should, since Snum $-\rangle$ Sname. The other FD's should be verified in a similar manner. The reader should also note that in the instance of ADVISOR given in Figure 2.5, only one Snum is associated with each Sname; however, this does not prove that Sname $-\rangle$ Snum, which is false. It only indicates that at the current time there are no two advisees with the same name. At some future date, it may be that two students with the same name will appear in ADVISOR.

3.3 BOYCE CODD NORMAL FORM (BCNF)

A skilled database designer can look at the diagram in Figure 3.2(b) and determine that the ADVISOR relation is not a "good" relation. The designer does this by looking at the FD's that are given for ADVISOR, and by noting that they have some undesirable properties. To discuss these undesirable properties, two terms related to FD's must be defined.

1. **Candidate Key:** A candidate key is an attribute, or set of attributes, that could be used as the primary key for a given relation. The primary key is always a candidate key; however, there may be other candidate keys that could have been used as the primary key, but were not.

2. **Determinant:** If A $-\rangle$ B is an FD, and if B is not functionally dependent upon any subset of A, then A is said to be the determinant of B.

From Figure 3.2 it can be deduced that ADVISOR has only one candidate key, namely, the composite set of attributes $\langle$Snum,Class,Term$\rangle$.

This is determined by finding the minimum set of attribute values, which, if known, will determine the values of all other attributes in a tuple. Using the FD's in Figure 3.2, it can be seen that Snum alone determines Sname, Rnum, and Pnum; and, to determine Grade the composite set Snum, Class, and Term must all be known. Thus, if the attribute values for the candidate key given above are known, the values for all other attributes in the tuple containing that candidate key will be uniquely specified.

The determinants in ADVISOR are easy to identify: they are the left-hand sides of all the FD's in the relation. The determinants in ADVISOR are ⟨Snum,Class,Term⟩, ⟨Snum⟩, ⟨Rnum⟩, and ⟨Pnum⟩. The determinants have been placed inside of ⟨ ⟩'s to emphasize that there are four different determinants. Note that mutual dependencies yield two determinants.

In one of the earliest, and one of the most important, discoveries in the area of relational database design, E. F. Codd proved that a majority of the potential anomalies in a database will be removed if every relation in the database has been properly decomposed into **Boyce Codd Normal Form** (BCNF). BCNF is defined as follows:

> A relation is in Boyce Codd Normal Form if, and only if, every determinant in the relation is a candidate key.

Although there are higher normal forms which force even more restrictions on the relations being developed, in practice, most designers try to get their relations into BCNF. This will be the goal in this text.

The ADVISOR relation is not in BCNF. This can be seen by listing all of the determinants, and all of the candidate keys, side by side, and noting if every determinant is a candidate key:

Candidate Keys of ADVISOR	Determinants of ADVISOR
⟨Snum,Class,Term⟩	⟨Snum,Class,Term⟩
	⟨Snum⟩
	⟨Pnum⟩
	⟨Rnum⟩

Since every determinant in ADVISOR is not a candidate key, ADVISOR is not in BCNF and should therefore be decomposed.

3.4 GENERAL APPROACH TO DECOMPOSITION

At this point the stage has been set for the presentation of an outline of one method that states how relational database design via **decomposition** should proceed. (It will be shown later that this method will have to be refined in order to overcome some further difficulties.)

1. Develop the universal relation for the database.
2. Determine all FD's related to the attributes in the relation.
3. Determine if the relation is in BCNF. If it is, the design is finished; if it isn't, the relation must be decomposed into two relations.
4. Repeat steps (2) and (3) for each new relation obtained by decomposition. When all relations are in BCNF, the design is complete.

The method proposed above does not define how a non-BCNF relation is to be decomposed into two relations. This is accomplished using FD's in the following manner.

> Take a relation, R(A,B,C,D,E,..), that is not in BCNF. Find an FD, C −⟩ D, which is known to be an FD that is causing R to not be in BCNF. (C is a determinant, but is not a candidate key.) Form two new relations: R1(A,B,C,E,..) and R2(C,D), where the dependency part of the FD has been dropped from R to form R1, and the full FD has been used to form R2. R1 and R2 must now be checked to see if they are in BCNF. R2(C,D) is said to be a **projection** out of R. This type of decomposition is said to be a **non-loss decomposition** under a natural join (see Appendix B for a discussion of this feature). This decomposition method can be used in Step 3 of the design algorithm listed above.

As an example of how the method is used, the ADVISOR relation will be decomposed. Looking back at the determinants and candidate keys for ADVISOR, it can be seen that there are three determinants that are not candidate keys:

⟨Snum⟩, ⟨Pnum⟩, and ⟨Rnum⟩

To start the process, the universal relation is defined as

ADVISOR (Snum, Class, Term, Sname, Rnum, Pnum, Grade)

The FD's that are candidates for projection are

Snum −⟩ Rnum; Snum −⟩ Pnum; Rnum −⟩ Pnum and Pnum −⟩ Rnum

At this point a decision has to be made as to which FD should be used for the first projection. It may be that different databases will result from different initial projections. If this is the case, each of the resulting databases would have to be inspected to see which one best fits the needs of the enterprise. A simple rule of thumb to use in picking the FD for projection is to look for a "chain" of FD's of the form

$$A \rightarrow B \rightarrow C$$

and then project out the rightmost FD. In this case, Snum $\rightarrow$ Rnum $\rightarrow$ Pnum form such a "chain," so the "end of the chain," Rnum $\rightarrow$ Pnum, will be projected out first. The resulting relations, R1 and R2, are given in Figure 3.3, along with each of their associated FD's.

Relation R2(Rnum,Pnum) is in BCNF, since in this relation all determinants are candidate keys. R2 needs no more reduction. However, R1(Snum,Class,Term,Sname,Rnum,Grade) is not in BCNF, since the determinant ⟨Snum⟩ is not a candidate key. R1 needs to be reduced further.

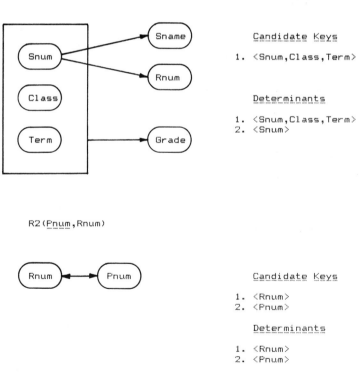

Figure 3.3 Relations R1 and R2 from the projection of Rnum ⟨ – ⟩ Pnum from ADVISOR.

The determinant that is causing the problem, ⟨Snum⟩, has two attributes dependent upon it,

$$Snum \rightarrow Sname$$
$$Snum \rightarrow Rnum$$

which can be thought of as a single FD with a composite right-hand side:

$$Snum \rightarrow Sname,Rnum$$

This is the FD that was projected out of R1 to give the relations R3 and R4 shown in Figure 3.4. These two relations are in BCNF and, along with R2, would be used to form the database for the advisor. Figure 3.5 gives the final relations for the database (called Adv database), along with instances of each relation that hold the same data given for the original AD-

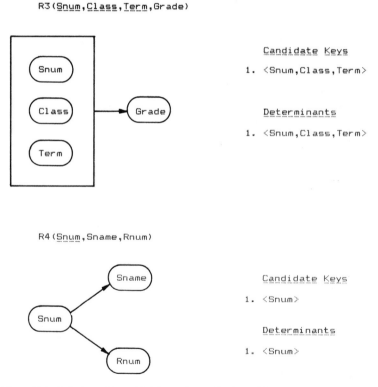

Figure 3.4 Relations R3 and R4 from the projection of Snum → Sname,Rnum from R1.

R2(Rnum,Pnum)
R3(Snum,Class,Term,Grade)
R4(Snum,Sname,Rnum)

(a)

R3

Snum	Class	Term	Grade
3215	MTH122	F84	1.6
3215	SCI120	F84	2.4
3215	PHY230	W85	2.1
3215	MTH122	W85	2.3
3462	MTH122	W84	2.3
3462	MTH123	W85	3.5
3462	PSY220	W85	3.7
3567	SCI239	W84	3.3
3567	EGR171	F84	3.5
3567	PHY141	F84	1.8
4756	MUS389	F83	4.0

R2

Rnum	Pnum
120DH	2136
238VH	2344
345VH	3321

R4

Snum	Sname	Rnum
3215	JonesG	120DH
3262	SmithA	238VH
3567	HowesJ	120DH
4756	AlexK	345VH

(b)

Figure 3.5   (a) The Adv database and (b) an instance of the database using the data from Figure 2.5.

VISOR relation. Note, in particular, that the decomposition process has automatically broken the original ADVISOR relation into three logical units: R2 has room and phone information; R3 has class and grade information; and R4 contains student information. This logical breakdown is a direct result of the use, during decomposition, of the information in the FD's that detailed how the various attributes in the original relation were related to one another.

3.5 REVIEW OF THE ORIGINAL ANOMALIES

A good question to ask at this point is: "Does the Adv database still have the anomalies that were present in the ADVISOR relation, or did the decomposition automatically remove the anomalies?" To show that the anomalies were removed, which is why the decomposition was done in the first place, the insertion, deletion, and update problems from Section 2.2 will be reviewed using the Adv database in Figure 3.5.

Insertion: When the ADVISOR relation was used for the database, a new student could not be added to the database until that student had actually completed a class. In the Adv database, general information on advisees is kept in relation R4. As long as the new student has been accepted at the university, and has been assigned a room, that student can be added to the database (in R4). The student doesn't even have to be taking a class in order to be entered into the database. The original insertion anomaly has been removed by decomposition.

Update: When the ADVISOR relation was used for the database, a problem resulted when Ms. G. Jones had her advisor change her phone number to 7777. The change resulted in two different phone numbers appearing in the database for the phone in room 120DH. In the Adv database, phone numbers are in relation R2, and each room can have only one phone number associated with the phone that is in that room. (Remember that Rnum is the primary key for R2, and primary key values by definition have to be unique.) To modify Ms. G. Jones' phone number, the tuple in R2 for Rnum = 120DH would be modified so that Pnum = 7777. Note that this changes the phone number in the room, so that all students living in that room would have their phone numbers changed also. Thus, the original update anomaly has been removed by the BCNF design.

It must again be pointed out that the removal of the update design anomaly is predicated upon the fact that the DBMS, upon which the database will be implemented, will not allow duplicate primary key values. Unfortunately, many microcomputer-based DBMS's will allow duplicate key values to occur, and it is the burden of the user, through proper programming methods, to make certain that duplicates don't occur. This is a case where a good database design can be ruined by the limitations of the DBMS being used. A fully implemented DBMS will not allow duplicate primary key values.

Deletion: When the ADVISOR relation was used as the database, the deletion of the tuple involving Snum = 4756 and Class = MUS389 eliminated student number 4756 from the database. This can't happen in the Adv database, since grade information and general student information are in two different relations (R3 and R4). To delete the fact that the student with number 4756 hadn't taken MUS389 in the F83 term, the tuple ⟨4756,MUS389,F83,4.0⟩ would be deleted from R3. This would have no effect on the general information on this student, which is stored in R4.

All three of the anomalies that were present in the single relation database have been removed by the new design. The cost of removing the anomalies is that three relations, rather than one, now need to be stored. This means that the queries that will be written to obtain information from the

```
. USE ADVISOR
. DISPLAY CLASS, GRADE FOR SNUM = 3462 OFF
MTH122   2.3
MTH123   3.5
PSY220   3.7
.
```

(a)

```
. USE R3
. DISPLAY CLASS, GRADE FOR SNUM = 3462 OFF
MTH122   2.3
MTH123   3.5
PHY220   3.7
.
```

(b)

Figure 3.6   dBase II queries to list the grades of all classes taken by student number 3462: (a) using the ADVISOR relation; (b) using the Adv database.

```
. USE ADVISOR
. DISPLAY PNUM FOR SNUM = 3567 OFF
2136
2136
2136
.
```

(a)

```
. SELECT PRIMARY
. USE R4
. SELECT SECONDARY
. USE R2
. JOIN TO TEMP1 FIELDS S.PNUM FOR P.SNUM = 3567 .AND. ;
P.RNUM = S.RNUM
. USE TEMP1
. LIST OFF
2136
. USE
. DELETE FILE TEMP1
FILE HAS BEEN DELETED
.
```

(b)

Figure 3.7   dBASE II queries to list the phone number of student number 3567: (a) using the ADVISOR relation; (b) using the Adv database.

database may end up being more complex, since they may have to link through two or three relations to find the data desired.

Figures 3.6 and 3.7 are examples of typical queries using dBASE II on both the single ADVISOR relation, and on the Adv database. In Figure 3.7 the queries using the Adv database case are more complex than those in the single relation case.[1]

---

[1]Those not familiar with the JOIN operator used in Figure 3.7 should review the material in Appendix A.

3.6 A DIFFERENT DECOMPOSITION
OF THE ADVISOR RELATION

In Section 3.5 the decomposition of the ADVISOR relation into three relations began with a projection of the FD

$$Rnum \; -\rangle \; Pnum$$

This FD was chosen because it was the last FD in the chain of FD's found
in Figure 3.2:

$$Snum \; -\rangle \; Rnum \; -\rangle \; Pnum$$

Careful study of the FD's given in Figure 3.2 shows that another chain of
FD's, with the same number of FD's involved, is present in Figure 3.2. This
chain is

$$Snum \; -\rangle \; Pnum \; -\rangle \; Rnum$$

The rightmost FD here is Pnum $-\rangle$ Rnum. If this FD had been projected
out of ADVISOR first, the resulting BCNF database would have been:

$$R2(Pnum,Rnum)$$
$$R3(\underline{Snum},Class,Term,Grade)$$
$$R4(\underline{Snum},Sname,Pnum)$$

This database is as valid as the one given in Figure 3.5. The only difference
is that Pnum has assumed a role superior to Rnum. Pnum is now the primary key for R2 (rather than Rnum), and the attribute that links R4 with
R2 is also Pnum (rather than Rnum). The two different database solutions
to the same problem are a direct result of the **mutual dependency** that exists
between Pnum and Rnum. Which one of the two solutions is "best" is
really a designer's choice, and will depend to some extent on how the advisor plans to use the database.

3.7 COMMENTS ON THE DECOMPOSITION
DESIGN ALGORITHM

It was stated in Section 3.4, that during the design process via projection,
decomposition should proceed by looking for a chain of FD's, e.g.,

$$A \; -\rangle \; B \quad \quad B \; -\rangle \; C$$

and then projecting out the FD at the end of the chain. In this case, B $-\rangle$ C would be the first FD projected. A different way to explain this selection process is to state that *every effort should be made to avoid projecting out an FD, when the dependency part of that FD is itself, either all, or part of, a determinant for another FD.*

In the case above, if the relation under discussion is taken as R(A,B,C), and if the FD A $-\rangle$ B were chosen to be projected out first, the resulting relations would be R1(A,C) and R2(A,B). Although both of these relations are in BCNF, there is a distinct problem:

> Neither relation R1(A,C), nor R2(A,B), by itself, contains the attributes in the FD, B $-\rangle$ C, which is an FD in the original relation. This FD was effectively lost in the design process. From a practical standpoint, this means that if the R1 and R2 given here were used for the database, there would be no assurance that incorrect relationships between B and C would not be entered into the database. Figure 3.8 illustrates the problem. By joining R1 and R2 over A, two values of C (3 and 4) can be related to B, which violates the FD that was lost in the projection process.

The problem in this example arose because of the projection of an FD, where the dependency portion of the FD was, itself, a determinant for another FD. This problem would not have resulted if the chain rule had been used.

Another case where an FD might be lost during the design process is the situation where one attribute is dependent upon two different determinants. Take the case of R(A,B,C) with the dependencies as shown in Figure 3.9. The relation R(A,B,C) is not in BCNF, since the only candidate key is $\langle$A,C$\rangle$, while the determinants are $\langle$A$\rangle$ and $\langle$C$\rangle$. The chain rule here isn't applicable, since there is no chain. Additionally, if either of the FD's is projected out in the normal manner, the other FD will be lost. For example, if A $-\rangle$ B is projected out of R(A,B,C) the resulting relations will be R1(A,C) and R2(A,B), with neither relation housing the FD C $-\rangle$ B. On the other hand, if C $-\rangle$ B is projected out first, then the FD A $-\rangle$ B will be lost. This is a case where the designer should consider splitting R(A,B,C) into R1(A,B) and R2(C,B), so that neither FD is lost. This does not follow the standard method of decomposition, but it might result in the best design. The only thing that a designer can do, when faced with the situation given here, is to check the three possible sets of design relations and see which set best fits the needs of the enterprise. In particular, the relations obtained in the last alternative must be checked to see if a join of the two resulting relations will cause any problems with retrievals when the final database is used.

The alternate method of splitting a relation, discussed in conjunction with Figure 3.9, is based on a design approach that is different from de-

ORIGINAL DATA:

Relation: R(A,B,C)

FD's: A -> B
        B -> C

(A -> C must also be true.)

ONE POSSIBLE DESIGN

R1(A,C)   R2(A,B)

A -> C   A -> B

Valid Instances of R1 and R2

R1

A	C
9	4
8	3

R2

A	B
9	2
8	2

The JOIN of R1 and R2

A	B	C
9	2	4
8	2	3

Figure 3.8   Instances of relations that satisfy FD's in R1 and R2, but violate an FD in the original specifications.

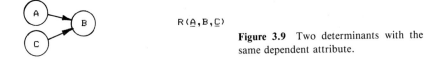

R(A,B,C)

Figure 3.9   Two determinants with the same dependent attribute.

composition, but is one that is used by many database designers. This approach, called by some the **synthesis method,** states (in its most simple form) that all FD's with exactly the same determinant should be separated into groups, and each group placed into its own relation. The resulting relations are then checked for BCNF. In the last example there were two FD's, each with a different determinant. Under the synthesis method, each FD would be placed into its own relation, giving R1(A,B) and R2(C,B). The synthesis design method can be used either by itself or in conjunction with the decomposition method. This text will use the decomposition method (also referred to as the projection method), with synthesis used as a possible alternative to get out of undesirable situations like the one above. As will be shown in Chapter 5, the dependency situations, similar to that given in Figure 3.9, can arise in real-world situations.

The indication above that there are several design methods, which may be used alone, or mixed to some extent, points out the fact that database design is part science and part art! The fact that several legitimate designs can be evolved from the same starting point is a fact of life in database design. Part of the design process is the evaluation of several design alternatives, to see which one best fits the needs of the enterprise.

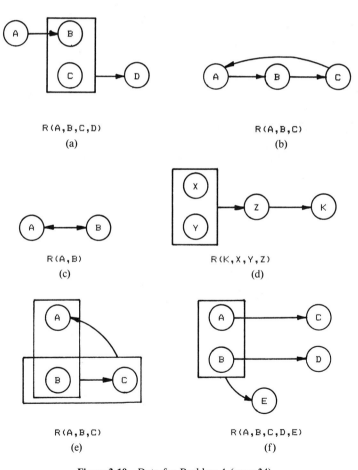

R(A,B,C,D)
(a)

R(A,B,C)
(b)

R(A,B)
(c)

R(K,X,Y,Z)
(d)

R(A,B,C)
(e)

R(A,B,C,D,E)
(f)

Figure 3.10   Data for Problem 1 (page 34).

3.8 PROBLEMS FOR CHAPTER 3

1. Figure 3.10 gives the functional dependency diagrams for several relations. For each relation, identify all determinants and all candidate keys. Determine which relations are in BCNF. If a relation is not in BCNF, reduce it to normal form using the decomposition algorithm.

2. Determine the functional dependencies between the attributes of the PHONE relation discussed in Problem 4 at the end of Chapter 2.

3. The Marty Mason Department Store wishes to develop a database to store information on customer accounts. The items to be stored in the database include the following for each customer: account number, name, address, phone number, credit rating (excellent, good, poor, bad), and balance due. Draw a functional dependency diagram for the attributes involved, listing the assumptions being used. Develop the BCNF relations for the database.

4. The Secretary of State's office is developing a database to store information on all automobiles registered in the state. Items to be stored in the database include registration number, license plate number, make of auto, owner of the auto, owner's address, name of the insurance company that insures the auto, insurance policy number, county in which the auto is registered, and date on which the auto was last registered. Develop the functional dependency diagram for the attributes involved.

4

SOME
DESIGN ALGORITHM
MODIFICATIONS

4.1 REDUNDANT FUNCTIONAL DEPENDENCIES

The database design algorithm outlined in Section 3.4 appears, on the surface, to be fairly straightforward; however, it does have some hidden problems. One problem is that the decomposition process can be complicated by the presence of redundant FD's.

A **redundant FD** is one that contains no information that cannot be obtained from the other FD's in the set being used to design the database. Since a redundant FD contains no unique information, it can be deleted from the set of FD's being used in the design process, without harmfully affecting the results. The redundant FD's are removed at the start of the design process, before the decomposition algorithm is applied.

4.2 TRANSITIVE DEPENDENCIES

One of the simplest ways that a redundant FD may appear in a set of FD's is when the FD has been generated through the concept of transitive dependency. **Transitive dependency** is defined as follows:

If A $-\rangle$ B and B $-\rangle$ C, then A $-\rangle$ C is a transitive dependency.

Two points need to be made here. First, the transitive dependency A −⟩ C, given in the definition above, is a valid dependency. There is nothing illegal about it. Second, if A −⟩ B, and B −⟩ C and A −⟩C are all part of a set of FD's, then A −⟩ C is redundant and does not need to be used in the design process. Indeed, the transitive dependency, A −⟩ C, will cause more harm than good during the design process, and should be eliminated from the set of design FD's before decomposition begins.

Figure 4.1 is an example of how a set of FD's can be simplified by removing transitive FD's. Figure 4.1(a) is assumed to be the original set of FD's that were present at the start of the design process. Figure 4.1(d) is the set of nonredundant FD's that were obtained by removing all transitive dependencies from the original set. Figure 4.2 shows the decomposition into a set of BCNF relations.

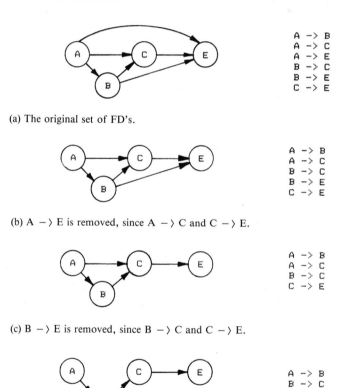

(a) The original set of FD's.

(b) A −⟩ E is removed, since A −⟩ C and C −⟩ E.

(c) B −⟩ E is removed, since B −⟩ C and C −⟩ E.

(d) A −⟩ C is removed, since A −⟩ B and B −⟩ C, giving the non-redundant set of FD's.

Figure 4.1   Removing transitive dependencies.

1. The FD diagram with no redundant FDs.

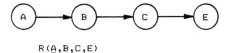

R(A,B,C,E)

2. Project out C — ⟩ E, since it is the end of a chain of dependencies.

R1 (C,E)

R2 (A,B,C)

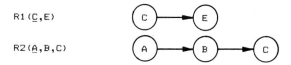

3. Project out B — ⟩ C from R2(A,B,C).

R1 (C,E)

R3 (B,C)

R4 (A,B)

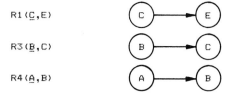

R1, R3, and R4 are all in BCNF. With a little practice, the BCNF relations in part 3 can be written down directly from part 1.

Figure 4.2   Reducing the relation from Figure 4.1 to a set of BCNF relations.

4.3 AUGMENTATION OF ATTRIBUTES IN AN FD

A second way that redundant FD's can be generated is through the concept of **augmentation.** This form of redundancy has several variations, and only the two simplest, but very useful, forms will be discussed here.

Variation one can be stated as follows, where A, B, and Z are attributes, any of which may be composite:

If A — ⟩ B, then A,Z — ⟩ B is a valid, but redundant FD. Attribute Z has been augmented to determinant A, without adding any new information in the process.

A second variation of augmentation occurs when the same attribute is added to both sides of a given FD to form a new FD:

If A — ⟩ B, then A,Z — ⟩ B,Z is a valid, but redundant FD.

Figure 4.3 gives examples of both forms of augmentation.

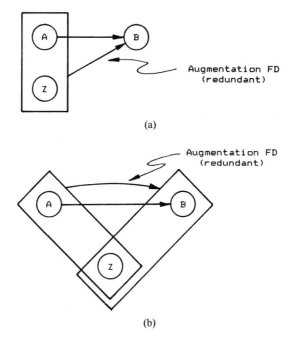

(a)

(b)

Figure 4.3   Examples of augmentation.

4.4 RULES OF INFERENCE

The definitions of transitive dependency and augmentation given above deal with only two of six rules of inference. These rules can be used to help reduce, or change, a given set of FD's into a different, but equivalent, set of FD's. Three more of these rules will be discussed briefly here. A complete discussion of all the rules of inference may be found in most of the more advanced database textbooks.

Two of the easiest rules of inference to understand deal with the union and decomposition of FD's. Union and decomposition are defined as

Union of FD's: If A $-\rangle$ B and A $-\rangle$ C, then A $-\rangle$ B,C.

Decomposition of FD's: If A $-\rangle$ B,C, then A $-\rangle$ B and A $-\rangle$ C.

Figure 4.4 gives a graphical representation of each one of these concepts, and Figure 4.5 shows how an original set of FD's can be reduced to a less complicated set of nonredundant FD's using the union, decomposition, and augmentation concepts.

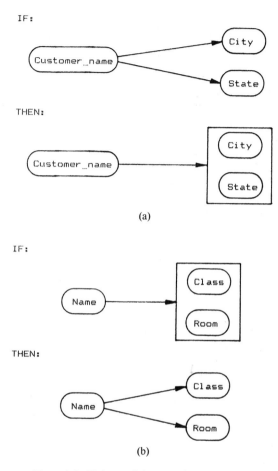

Figure 4.4 Union and decomposition examples.

The last rule of inference to be introduced is called **pseudotransitivity.**

If X −⟩ Y and Y,W −⟩ Z, then X,W −⟩ Z is redundant due to pseudo-transitivity.

A graphical example of pseudotransitivity is given in Figure 4.6. This type of redundancy arises in those cases where composite determinants are found in the FD's developed. A real-world example of this will be shown in the case study database in the next chapter.

For most people, the graphical forms of the dependency diagrams usually make it easier to spot redundant FD's; however, when the number of

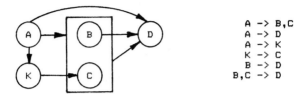

A -> B,C
A -> D
A -> K
K -> C
B -> D
B,C -> D

(a) The original set of FDs.

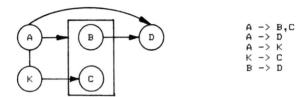

A -> B,C
A -> D
A -> K
K -> C
B -> D

(b) B,C —⟩ D is removed (augmentation with B —⟩ D).

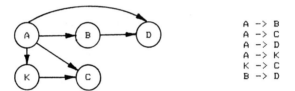

A -> B
A -> C
A -> D
A -> K
K -> C
B -> D

(c) A —⟩ B,C is replaced by A —⟩ B & A —⟩ C (decomposition).

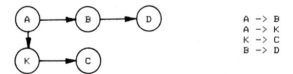

A -> B
A -> K
K -> C
B -> D

(d) A —⟩ C and A —⟩ D are removed by A —⟩ K & K —⟩ C and A —⟩ B & B —⟩ D (transitivity).

Figure 4.5 Reducing an FD diagram using rules of inference.

attributes and FD's involved becomes large, the graphical approach may be too cumbersome to handle. In this case, there are mathematical algorithms available to find the redundant FD's. These are not too hard to use, if you are mathematically inclined.

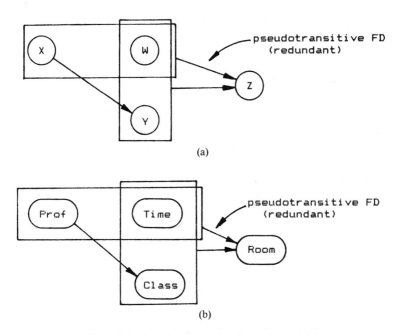

(a)

(b)

Figure 4.6   Graphical examples of pseudotransitivity.

4.5 MINIMAL COVER

A set of nonredundant FD's, which is obtained by removing all redundant FD's from a set of FD's using the six rules of inference, is termed a **minimal cover.** Unfortunately, the minimal cover may not be unique, since the order in which redundant FD's are removed from a set may have an effect on the minimal cover obtained. To show that the minimal cover may not be unique, the reader should verify that there are two minimal covers for the database design problem outlined in Figure 3.2. One minimal cover is obtained by removing the FD Snum − ⟩ Pnum from the original set, while the second minimal cover is obtained by removing the FD Snum − ⟩ Rnum. The use of these two minimal covers leads to the same two database designs discussed earlier. One final point should be emphasized with regard to the elimination of redundant FD's from a given set: redundant FD's should be removed one at a time, with the new set of FD's obtained after each elimination reevaluated to see if any redundant FD's are still present. This process is repeated until no redundant FD's are present, at which time the remaining set of FD's is a minimal cover.

4.6 REVISED DESIGN ALGORITHM

The following general design algorithm for decomposition will be used throughout the remainder of this text:

1. Develop the universal relation for the database.
2. Determine all FD's relating to the attributes in the universal relation.
3. Remove all redundant FD's from the original set of FD's to obtain a minimal cover. This must be accomplished by removing redundant FD's one at a time, and then checking the remaining set of FD's to see if any redundancies are still present.
4. Use the FD's in the minimal cover to decompose the universal relation into a set of BCNF relations. The Decomposition Algorithm given in Section 3.4 should be followed.
5. If more than one minimal cover can be obtained, compare the designs generated by each minimal cover to see which one best fits the needs of the enterprise.

In using the decomposition algorithm in Step 4, it should be remembered that an FD should not be projected when the dependency portion of the FD is, itself, a determinant for another FD; also, care must be exercised in those cases where the dependency portion of the FD is dependent upon more than one determinant. Either one of these cases can lead to the loss of an FD from the database. If a place is reached in the decomposition process where no more projections can be made without causing the loss of an FD, the designer should consider one of two options: (1) Take the remaining FD's and create one relation for each determinant and its set of dependent attributes; or (2) change the order of earlier decompositions, since the design algorithm doesn't yield unique solutions.

4.7 CHECKING THE PROPOSED FINAL
DESIGN RELATIONS

After a set of BCNF relations have been developed, and are being considered as the final design for the database, the set must be checked for possible problems.

1. Make a list of the FD's found in each relation. The lists should be checked in two ways: first, the same FD should not appear in more

than one relation; and second, the set of FD's from the proposed design relations should be exactly the same as the set of FD's found in the minimal cover that was present at the start of the design process. (If the design set of FD's is not exactly the same as the set in the minimal cover, you should be able to show that you can obtain the design set from the minimal cover, using the rules of inference.) If either of these checks fails, the design should be checked for errors and/or other designs considered.

2. Check to see if any of the relations are redundant. A relation is redundant if: (a) all the attributes in the redundant relation can be found in one other relation in the design set; or (b) all the attributes in the redundant relation can be found in a relation that can be generated from other relations in the proposed design set through a series of JOIN operations on those relations. If a relation is found to be redundant, it should be dropped from the design set. Examples of both types of redundant relations are given below.

   As an example of the first type, assume that the proposed set of design relations is

$$R1(A,B)$$
$$R2(\overline{B},C,Y,Z)$$
$$R3(\overline{A},B,K)$$

R1 is redundant, since all of its attributes can be found in R3.

   As an example of the second type, assume that the proposed set of design relations is

$$R1(A,C,X)$$
$$R3(\overline{D},K,F)$$
$$R5(\overline{D},E,G,H)$$
$$R7(\overline{A},B,D)$$
$$R8(\overline{A},\overline{B},E,G)$$

R8 is redundant, since a JOIN of R5 and R7 (using common attribute D) gives a relation R9(A,B,D,E,G,H), which contains all of the attributes that are in R8.

3. Look at the relations from a practical standpoint. Visualize how the relations will be used in the final database, and determine if they will support the type of query and update operations that will be used.

4.8 PROBLEMS FOR CHAPTER 4

1. Place each functional dependency found in Figure 4.7 into mathematical form in the manner shown in Figure 4.1. Next, reduce the diagram in a step-by-step manner by eliminating all transitive dependencies.
2. Identify all of the FD's in Figure 4.8 that are redundant due to augmentation.
3. In Figure 4.9, can the diagram on the right be obtained from the diagram on the left using the rules of inference given in this chapter?

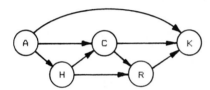

Figure 4.7 Functional dependency diagram for Problem 1.

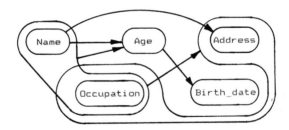

Figure 4.8   Functional dependency diagram for Problem 2.

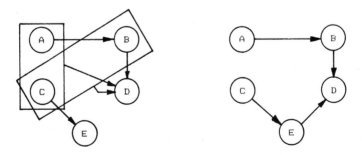

Figure 4.9   Functional dependency diagram for Problem 3.

4. Assume that a design gives the following four BCNF relations:
R1(<u>Emp-name</u>, Emp-address, Age, Sex, Supervisor-name)
R2(<u>Supervisor-name</u>, Department)
R3(<u>Emp-name</u>, Department)
R4(<u>Department</u>, Dept-Phone-no, Dept-address)
One of the relations is redundant. Identify the relation and discuss why
it is redundant.

5. If the relations given in Problem 4 are in BCNF, which of the following
statements must be true, and which ones must be false? Explain your
reasoning.
   a) An employee can work for more than one supervisor.
   b) An employee works for only one department.
   c) A department has only one phone.
   d) A department has only one phone number.
   e) Each supervisor has a phone.
   f) Employees who are not supervisors do not have phones.

5

CASE STUDY
OF A DATABASE DESIGN

A database is to be designed for use by the secretary of a bowling league in a small midwestern town. The secretary will store all data that are pertinent to the league in the database, and will generate weekly reports about the league using the DBMS. A special report will be generated at the end of the season. The database will be implemented using both dBASE III and R:base 5000. A complete description of the data that the secretary wishes to have available for the reports is detailed in the following paragraphs.

5.1 DESCRIPTION OF THE PROBLEM

The bowling secretary will need the name, phone number, and address of each bowler in the league. Since the league is limited to residents of the town, the town name and ZIP code for each bowler will not have to be stored. The weekly game scores for all three games bowled by each bowler and the current average for each bowler will be of interest. The secretary will need to know the name of the team for which each bowler bowls, and the name of the captain of each team. In addition to having a name, the secretary plans to assign each team a unique team number.

The starting average of each bowler will be required, since this will be used to determine both the "most improved bowler" in the league at the end of the season, and the handicap for each bowler for the first week of the season. Each bowler's high game and high series will be required for the presentation of awards at the end of the season.

The secretary plans to include in the weekly report information on each bowler's total pins and total games, which are used to calculate their current average and current handicap. The handicap used by the league is 75 percent of the difference between 200 and the bowler's average, with no negative handicaps allowed. If the handicap calculation results in a fraction, that fraction will be truncated. The handicap is recalculated each week.

Lane assignments, indicating the lane to which each team is assigned each week, are required. Teams sharing a common ball return will be opponents, so this information does not have to be stored in the database.

Finally, the database must contain all the information necessary for the calculation of team standings. A team scores one win for each game in which the team knocks down more pins (including handicap pins) than their opponents. Likewise, a team will get one loss for each game in which the team knocks down fewer pins than their opponents. A team also scores one win (loss) for having more (fewer) total pins than their opponents in the three games rolled each week. Thus, four team points (won or lost) are scored each week of the season. Each team is given half-a-win and half-a-loss in those cases where a tie occurs. If a team has more than two members absent on a given evening, that team automatically receives four losses, and their opponents get the four wins. The defaulting team does not accumulate any pins in total team pins, even if the remaining bowlers bowl; however, the remaining bowlers' pins and games will accumulate on their individual records.

5.2 DETERMINING THE UNIVERSAL RELATION ATTRIBUTES

After several discussion sessions with the secretary, the following attributes, and restrictions on them, were deemed to be prime candidates for the universal relation. Each attribute is shown with both a short descriptive name suitable for use in the database implementation, and a shorter two-character form that can be used in the FD diagrams. The two character versions were chosen to make the FD diagrams less cumbersome to present, while still maintaining some mnemonic form of where the attribute originated.

Attribute		Comments
Nb:	Tnumb	A team number. Teams are numbered consecutively beginning with the number 1.
Tn:	Tname	A team name. Each team in the league has a name, e.g., "PinBusters." Names are unique.
Bn:	Bname	A bowler's name. Since it is a small league, it is assumed that no two bowlers will have exactly the same name.
Av:	Bavg	A given bowler's average. This is the average pins/game for all games bowled to date. The average will be truncated to a whole number.
Hk:	Hndk	A bowler's per game handicap. This is an integer value that is recalculated each week.
Bg:	Bgame	The total number of games that a bowler has bowled to date. A bowler normally bowls three games/night.
Wn:	Wins	Total number of wins for a given team for the season.
Ls:	Loss	Total number of losses for a given team for the season.
Tp:	Tpins	Total number of pins for a given team for the season.
Ln:	Lane	The number of the lane to which a given team is assigned on a given week. This number also determines the opponent for that week. Teams on lanes 1 and 2 are opponents as are teams on lanes 3 and 4, etc.
Cp:	Captn	Name of the team captain. There is only one captain per team.
Ph:	Phone	Phone number of a bowler. More than one bowler may have the same phone number.
St:	Stret	Street address of a bowler. All addresses are in the same small town. More than one bowler may live at the same address.
Bp:	Bpins	The total of all pins for a given bowler for the season.
Sa:	Stavg	The average that a given bowler had at the start of the season. This is an integer value. (*Cont'd.*)

Attribute		Comments
Hg:	Higam	Score of the highest game bowled by a given bowler during the season.
Hs:	Hiser	Score of the highest three-game series for a given bowler during the season.
Wk:	Week	Number of weeks into the season. This value starts at 1 and increases by 1 for each week of the season.
G1:	Game1	Score of the first game bowled on a given week by a given bowler.
G2:	Game2	Score of the second game bowled on a given week by a given bowler.
G3:	Game3	Score of the third game bowled on a given week by a given bowler.

After some thought, it was decided that several of the attributes listed should not be stored in the database. The ones eliminated were Bavg, Bgame, Wins, Loss, Tpins, Bpins, Hndk, Higam, and Hiser. Although these are all items that will appear in both the weekly and the year-end reports, their values can be calculated from other attributes that will be stored in the database.

If the items listed for elimination were stored in the database, they would represent a type of redundant information that would lead to severe update problems. For example, assume that all of the items listed for elimination were actually stored in the database, and that an error was found in the entry of a game score for one bowler. A change in the bowler's score on this one game would require a certain change in both Bpins and Tpins, with possible changes required in all the other items listed for elimination. If these secondary changes were not all made, the database would be inconsistent. For this reason, the items listed for elimination will not be stored in the database, but will be calculated from data in the database whenever a report is needed. These calculations will be made using special software application programs that will be written using the macro language of the DBMS. These macros will be given in Chapters 9 and 10.

Step 1 of the revised design algorithm given in Section 4.5 is the determination of the universal relation for the database being designed. When the final list of attributes to be used in the bowling secretary's database are grouped together into one relation, the universal relation can be formally defined as

$$R(Nb,Tn,Bn,Ln,Cp,Ph,St,Sa,Wk,G1,G2,G3)$$

5.3 THE FUNCTIONAL DEPENDENCY DIAGRAM

Step 2 of the revised design algorithm is the determination of all of the FD's relating the attributes in the universal relation. Figure 5.1 gives the functional dependency diagram for the universal relation that was deduced from the problem as stated.

Step 3 of the revised design algorithm calls for the removal of all redundant FD's from the set of FD's defined for the universal relation, in order to obtain a minimal cover. The FD's, shown diagrammatically in Figure 5.1, contain several transitive dependencies. (Other transitive dependencies could easily have been generated in an original set of FD's. Typical transitive dependencies that might have arisen are listed in Figure 5.1 as having already been eliminated. These were not included in the FD diagram

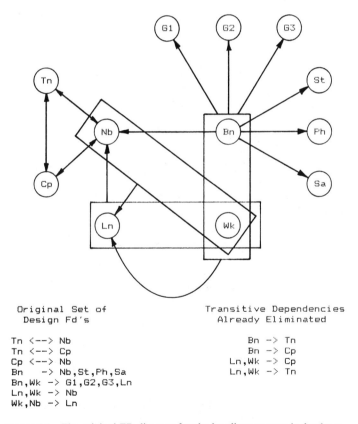

```
Original Set of              Transitive Dependencies
Design Fd's                  Already Eliminated

Tn <--> Nb                        Bn -> Tn
Tn <--> Cp                        Bn -> Cp
Cp <--> Nb                      Ln,Wk -> Cp
Bn    -> Nb,St,Ph,Sa            Ln,Wk -> Tn
Bn,Wk -> G1,G2,G3,Ln
Ln,Wk -> Nb
Wk,Nb -> Ln
```

Figure 5.1   The original FD diagram for the bowling secretary's database.

strictly for ease of presentation. These redundant dependencies could have been eliminated in any order.)

An out-of-the-ordinary transitive redundancy situation involves the "circular set of mutual dependencies" between the three attributes Cp, Nb, and Tn:

$$Nb \langle - - \rangle Cp$$
$$Cp \langle - - \rangle Tn$$
$$Tn \langle - - \rangle Nb$$

If any one of these three mutual dependencies is eliminated, the remaining two will not be redundant. In this particular case it makes no difference which one of the three mutual dependencies is deleted, since, regardless of the choice, the three attributes Cp, Nb, and Tn will still end up in the same relation, and all three will be candidate keys for that relation. The mutual dependency that was dropped is Cp $\langle - - \rangle$ Tn.

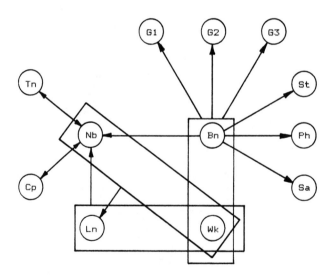

R(Nb,B̲n̲,Ln,Cp,Ph,St,Sa,W̲k̲,G1, G2,G3)

```
FD's:   Nb <--> Tn
        Nb <--> Cp
        Wk,Ln -> Nb
        Wk,Nb -> Ln
        Bn,Wk -> G1,G2,G3
        Bn -> Nb,St,Ph,Sa
```

Figure 5.2   The minimal cover FD diagram for the bowling secretary's database.

A second redundant FD found in Figure 5.1 is due to pseudotransitivity. Since Bn $-\rangle$ Nb and Nb,Wk $-\rangle$ Ln, it follows from pseudotransitivity that Bn,Wk $-\rangle$ Ln. This means that the last FD is redundant and can be dropped from the set. No other redundant FD's are present in Figure 5.1. The FD diagram for the minimal cover is given in Figure 5.2.

5.4 REDUCTION TO A SET OF BCNF RELATIONS

Step 4 of the design process involves the reduction of the universal relation into a set of BCNF relations. The universal relation, R, whose FD diagram is shown in Figure 5.2, is not in BCNF. When the candidate keys and determinants in R are compared, it is found that they are not identical:

Candidate Keys in R	Determinants in R
⟨Bn,Wk⟩	⟨Bn⟩
	⟨Bn,Wk⟩
	⟨Ln,Wk⟩
	⟨Nb⟩
	⟨Tn⟩
	⟨Cp⟩

To begin the reduction of R, all FD's which have attribute Nb as the determinant are projected out of the universal relation. This involves the FD's

$$\text{Nb} \langle - - \rangle \text{Cp}$$
$$\text{Nb} \langle - - \rangle \text{Tn}$$

and gives relations R1 and R2 as shown in Figure 5.3 (p. 54).

R2 is in BCNF, since Cp, Nb, and Tn are the only determinants in R2, and each is a candidate key. R2 will thus be included as part of the final design. R1 is not in BCNF, since a comparison of the determinants and candidate keys shows that they are not identical:

Candidate Keys in R1	Determinants in R1
⟨Bn,Wk⟩	⟨Bn⟩
	⟨Bn,Wk⟩
	⟨Nb,Wk⟩
	⟨Ln,Wk⟩

R1 must be reduced. At this stage of the reduction process, care must be taken with regard to attribute Nb. Nb is a dependent attribute in R1 that has two different determinants. As was noted in Section 3.7, it is possible to lose an FD if the projection is made incorrectly. In fact, it may be im-

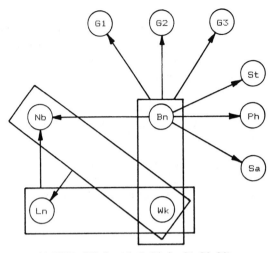

(a) R1(<u>Bn</u>,<u>Wk</u>,Ln,Nb,St,Ph,Sa,G1,G2,G3)

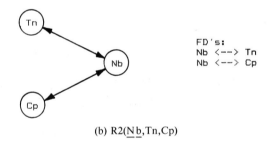

FD's:
Nb <--> Tn
Nb <--> Cp

(b) R2(<u>Nb</u>,Tn,Cp)

Figure 5.3   Results of projecting R2 from R.

possible to make a projection without losing an FD, which would mean that a design method other than decomposition would have to be considered.

The correct way to reduce R1 is to project out the FD Nb,Wk $-\rangle$ Ln to form R3 and R4 as given in Figure 5.4. This keeps both FD's with Nb as the dependent portion in the database: Bn $-\rangle$ Nb is in R3, and Ln,Wk $-\rangle$ Nb is in R4. R4 is in BCNF, but R3 is not.

Candidate Keys in R3	Determinants in R3
⟨Bn,Wk⟩	⟨Bn⟩
	⟨Bn,Wk⟩

R3 can be decomposed by projecting out all FD's with Bn as the determinant. This set of FD's is Bn $-\rangle$ Nb,St,Pn,Sa. The projection gives

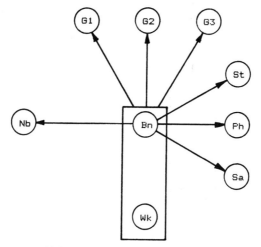

(a) R3(Bn,Wk,Nb,St,Ph,Sa,G1,G2,G3)

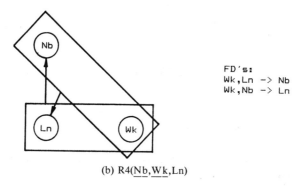

FD's:
Wk,Ln -> Nb
Wk,Nb -> Ln

(b) R4(Nb,Wk,Ln)

Figure 5.4   Results of projecting R4 from R1.

relations R5 and R6 as shown in Figure 5.5 (p. 56). Both R5 and R6 can be shown to be in BCNF. Thus the final design relations are R2, R4, R5 and R6.

5.5 EVALUATING THE BCNF DESIGN RELATIONS

The set of BCNF relations generated by the revised decomposition design algorithm, beginning with relation R in Figure 5.1, is

R2(Nb,Cp,Tn)
R4(Nb,Wk,Ln)
R5(Bn,Wk,G1,G2,G3)
R6(Bn,Nb,St,Ph,Sa)

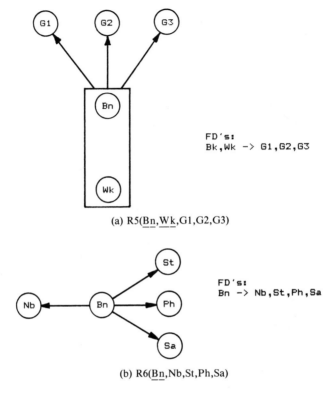

FD's:
Bk,Wk -> G1,G2,G3

(a) R5(B̲n̲,W̲k̲,G1,G2,G3)

FD's:
Bn -> Nb,St,Ph,Sa

(b) R6(B̲n̲,Nb,St,Ph,Sa)

Figure 5.5   Results of projecting R6 from R3.

where the primary key of each relation has been underlined. (Both R2 and R4 have more than one candidate key.) This set will now be checked for possible problems.

If the FD's found in the FD diagrams for each individual relation are listed,

Relation	Figure No.	FD's
R2	5.3	Tn ⟨ − ⟩ Nb
		Cp ⟨ − ⟩ Nb
R4	5.4	Wk,Ln − ⟩ Nb
		Wk,Nb − ⟩ Ln
R5	5.5	Bn,Wk − ⟩ G1,G2,G3
R6	5.5	Bn − ⟩ Nb,St,Ph,Sa

two things can be noted: (1) no FD appears more than once; and (2) the set of FD's here is the same as the set of FD's found in the minimal cover in Figure 5.2.

If the four relations are analyzed, no relation can be found where all of its attributes appear as a subset of the attributes in another relation. Additionally, there is no way to JOIN any three of design relations in a manner that will generate all of the attributes in the fourth relation. Thus, none of the four relations is redundant.

If the longer attribute names are used in place of the shorter two-character versions, the relations are

            R2(Tnumb, Captn, Tname)
            R4(Tnumb, Week, Lane)
            R5(Bname, Week, Game1, Game2, Game3)
            R6(Bname, Tnumb, Phone, Stret, Stavg)

By looking over the attributes contained in each relation, it can be seen that each relation houses a cohesive set of data:

            R2: Team information.
            R4: The season schedule.
            R5: Individual bowler scoring information.
            R6: Individual bowler personal information.

The relations appear to be quite reasonable from a practical standpoint.

Although the problem did not surface in this example, it is possible that, during the design process, attributes may be grouped together into relations in a rather nonsensical manner. The final design must always be checked to make certain that this is not the case. This problem is most apt to arise when the abbreviations used for the attributes are so short that the designer loses track of what the attribute names represent. A good designer looks at the attributes as they are being projected and tries to visualize whether they belong together.

The secretary's database will be implemented in dBASE III in Chapter 9, and in R:base 5000 in Chapter 10. Sample program modules will be given to generate some of the reports needed by the secretary.

5.6 PROBLEMS FOR CHAPTER 5

1. Redesign the bowling secretary's database under the assumption that the "calculable" attributes (Bavg, Bgame, Wins, Losses, Tpins, Bpins, Hndk, Higam, and Hiser) are to be stored in the database.
2. If the database from Problem 1 were implemented, how could the secretary be prevented from placing data into the database which would cause some of the calculated attributes to be in error?

6

A DIFFERENT
DESIGN APPROACH

The decomposition design approach discussed in the first five chapters of this book is a good one, provided there are not too many attributes involved. How many attributes and FD's that it takes to be considered too many is a matter of personal opinion; however, most people find that when the number of attributes exceeds twenty, the decomposition method can become rather cumbersome. In those cases where the number of attributes makes the decomposition method too difficult to handle, other design methods should be considered. One method that can be used in such cases is called the **Entity-Relationship Method.** This method differs from the decomposition method in that FD's become involved only at the end of the design process, rather than at the beginning.

6.1 ENTITIES AND RELATIONSHIPS

To gain a feeling for how the method works, a particular example will be investigated. Assume that a database is to be designed to hold information on university faculty members and the courses that they teach. The two main objects, or entities, of interest here are FACULTY and COURSE. These two entities are related, or associated, by the relationship TEACH, so we say (in rather poor English):

FACULTY   TEACH   COURSE

The relationship, TEACH, that exists between the two entities FACULTY and COURSE can be depicted graphically in several ways: only two will be discussed here. Figure 6.1 illustrates the use of an ER **occurrence diagram** with an example showing which faculty members teach exactly which courses. In this example, each faculty member is identified by a faculty_number (fno), and each course is identified by a course_number (cno). Figure 6.2 is called an ER **type diagram** and holds the same general information as is contained in Figure 6.1. Although it may not be apparent at the moment, Figure 6.2 contains all the information required to generate the first level design relations for the database.

Before proceeding further, some of the terminology being used must be clarified. Unfortunately, some of the terms used with the ER method can only be defined rather loosely, but they still must be defined.

ENTITY: An entity is defined as being a thing that is of interest to the enterprise. This thing must have occurrences that can be uniquely identified one from another. The only defining feature that may help in finding entities is that an entity is usually a noun. Examples of entities are machines, bank accounts, colleges, employees, and contracts. In Figures 6.1 and 6.2, the en-

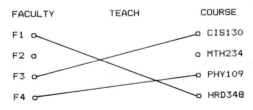

Figure 6.1 An example of an ER occurrence diagram.

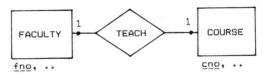

Figure 6.2 An example of an ER type diagram.

tities are COURSE and FACULTY, while individual occurrences of each entity are identified by course_number and faculty_number, respectively.

RELATIONSHIP: A relationship is an association, or connection, between two or more entities. The main aid in finding relationships is to note that a relationship is normally a verb. Typical examples of relationships between two entities are Employees WORK_FOR Departments, Students STUDY Subjects, and Workers MAINTAIN Machines.

Tied in with the concepts of entity and relationship is a third important concept which has been discussed before, called an attribute.

ATTRIBUTE: An attribute is a property of an entity. For instance, attributes that might be properties of the entity COURSE are course_number, section_number, rubric, term_in_which_offered, enrollment, and prerequisite.

The definitions for entity, relationship, and attribute are not very specific, but are good enough to use in the manner for which they are intended. One disconcerting fact, with respect to the ER method, is that two designers may view the same problem from different viewpoints, and end up with different sets of entities and relationships. The determination of which of the two sets is better may be strictly a matter of choice.

To further illustrate the forms of the graphical notation, note that in the ER occurrence diagram (Figure 6.1) each entity is named in capital letters above the entity occurrences, while each entity occurrence is identified by an attribute value. Thus COURSE is the entity and CIS130 is a specific entity occurrence. The relationship is also named and capitalized above the relationship occurrences, with each individual relationship occurrence specified with a line between the two entity occurrences it relates. The relationship occurrence that exists between CIS130 and F3, for instance, means that the faculty member whose faculty_number is F3 teaches the course with course_number CIS130.

In some cases it may take a composite set of attributes to identify each entity occurrence. The attribute, or set of attributes, used to identify an entity occurrence is termed the **entity key**. Each relationship occurrence can be uniquely identified by using the set of entity keys it relates. Thus, ⟨F3,CIS130⟩ is one **relationship key**. At this point in the design process, the only attributes required are those needed for the entity keys. Other attributes, and the FD's that are involved with them, will be added later in the design process.

In an ER type diagram, such as Figure 6.2, entities are identified with rectangles, while relationships are identified with diamond shapes. Below each entity is placed the attribute, or set of attributes, that is the entity key for that entity. The number "1" that appears in the ER type diagrams in

Figure 6.2, along with the small solid circles, will be discussed in the next section. In most cases, the ER type diagram is used to determine the set of relations for the database being designed, rather than the occurrence diagram.

6.2 THE DEGREE OF A RELATIONSHIP

An important aspect of a relationship between two, or more, entities is the **degree of the relationship.** This concept will be developed by expanding on the data depicted in Figure 6.1. Figure 6.3 shows all of the possible forms of ER occurrence diagrams that might exist between the entities FACULTY and COURSE, if the degree of the relationship is 1:1. Each diagram represents a different set of possible rules under which the enterprise (a university in this case) might operate. Only one of these occurrence diagrams could be correct for the enterprise at any point in time.

The set of rules that would have to hold for the different diagrams in Figure 6.3 to be true are as follows:

Figure 6.3(a): Each faculty member will teach no more than one course, and each course will be taught by no more than one faculty member. (The specific implication here is that there may be faculty who don't teach any courses, and there may be courses that aren't taught by any faculty member. Therefore, no faculty member will teach more than one course, and no course will be taught by more than one faculty member.)

Figure 6.3(b): Each faculty member teaches exactly one course, and each course will be taught by no more than one faculty member.

Figure 6.3(c): Each faculty member will teach no more than one course, and each course is taught by exactly one faculty member.

Figure 6.3(d): Each faculty member teaches exactly one course, and each course is taught by exactly one faculty member.

Since each entity occurrence on either side of the diagram connects with, at most, one entity occurrence on the opposite side of the diagram, each of the occurrence diagrams in Figure 6.3 are referred to as being of degree 1:1. The difference between the various diagrams in the figure deals with the situation as to whether or not every entity occurrence has to participate in the relationship. In Figure 6.3(a), not all of the entity occurrences from either entity have to participate in the relationship. In Figure 6.3(b),

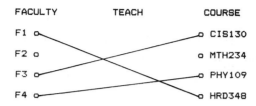

(a) Degree 1:1 with neither entity's membership obligatory

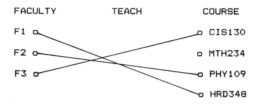

(b) Degree 1:1 with the FACULTY entity's membership obligatory

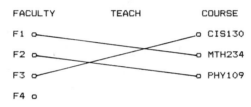

(c) Degree 1:1 with the COURSE entity's membership obligatory

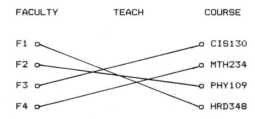

(d) Degree 1:1 with both entity's membership obligatory

Figure 6.3   Various membership classes with degree 1:1.

each faculty occurrence has to participate, while some of the course occurrences may not participate. In Figure 6.3(c), each course occurrence has to participate, while some faculty occurrences may not participate. In Figure 6.3(d), all entity occurrences of both entity types have to participate in the relationship.

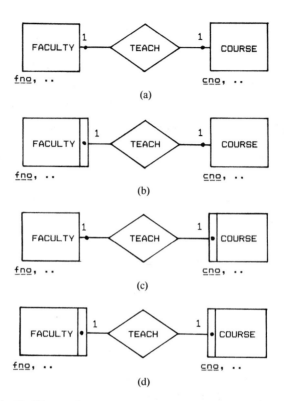

Figure 6.4 The ER type diagrams related to the ER occurrence diagrams in Figure 6.3.

Figure 6.4 shows how the information from Figure 6.3 can be placed into a more compact form. If the occurrences of a given entity have to participate in the relationship, the participation is said to be **obligatory,** and this fact is noted by placing a small solid circle in a box next to that entity. If the occurrences of a given entity do not have to participate in the relationship, the participation is said to be **nonobligatory,** and the solid circle is not placed inside a small box. The **membership class** of an entity must be either obligatory or nonobligatory, and is determined by the rules under which the enterprise operates. Since 1s' appear on both sides of the relationship in Figure 6.4, this means that the degree of the relationships are all 1:1. Degrees other than 1:1 are possible, and will be discussed later in this section.

In ER type diagrams, the entity key for each entity is listed, and underlined, immediately below each entity box: fno (faculty_number) for FACULTY, and cno (course_number) for COURSE. The dots that follow each of these attributes are placed there to indicate that, although other attributes may be involved with that particular entity, none of the additional attributes are part of the entity key. These other attributes will be added later, when the relations are developed.

The enterprise rules used to develop the diagrams in Figures 6.1 through 6.4 all had no faculty member teaching more than one course, and no course being taught by more than one faculty member. In most university settings this would not be the case. There are other sets of rules under which many universities operate.

CASE 1: Each faculty member may teach several courses, but each course is taught by, at most, one faculty member.

CASE 2: Each faculty member teaches, at most, one course, but each course may be taught by several faculty members.

CASE 3: Each faculty member may teach several courses, and each course may be taught by several faculty members.

Each of these cases has several variations: namely, the membership class can be obligatory, or nonobligatory, for either entity, for neither entity, or for both entities. The possible forms for each case will be studied one at a time. It turns out that cases 1 and 2 are symmetric in form.

Figure 6.5 (p. 66) shows the various occurrence diagrams related to CASE 1, while Figure 6.6 (p. 67) shows the equivalent type diagrams. In the (a) sections, the membership class of neither side is obligatory. In the (b) and (c) sections the membership class of only one side is obligatory. In the (d) sections the membership class of both sides is obligatory. In each of these sections, the degree of the relationship is termed 1:n (1 to n), due to each course occurrence being tied to, at most, one faculty occurrence (giving the 1), while each faculty occurrence can be tied to more than one course occurrence (giving the n).

Figure 6.7 (p. 68) shows the various occurrence diagrams related to CASE 2, while Figure 6.8 (p. 69) shows the equivalent type diagrams. In the (a) sections, the membership class of neither side is obligatory. In the (b) and (c) sections the membership class of only one side is obligatory. In the (d) sections the membership class of both sides is obligatory. In each of these sections, the degree of the relationship is termed n:1 (n to 1), since each course occurrence can be tied to more than one faculty occurrence (giving the n), while each faculty occurrence is tied to at most one course occurrence (giving the 1).

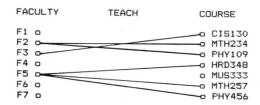

(a) Degree 1:n with neither entity's membership obligatory

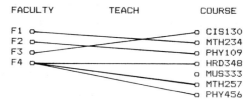

(b) Degree 1:n with the FACULTY entity's membership obligatory

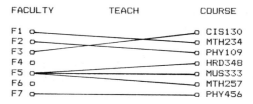

(c) Degree 1:n with the COURSE entity's membership obligatory

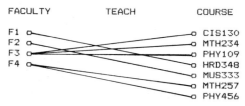

(d) Degree 1:n with both entity's membership obligatory

Figure 6.5 Examples of ER occurrence diagrams when the degree of the relationship is 1:n.

Figure 6.9 (p. 70) shows the various occurrence diagrams related to CASE 3, while Figure 6.10 (p. 71) shows the equivalent type diagrams. In the (a) sections, the membership class of neither side is obligatory. In the (b) and (c) sections the membership class of only one side is obligatory. In the (d) sections the membership class of both sides is obligatory. In each of these sections, the degree of the relationship is termed m:n (m to n), since each course occurrence can be tied to more than one faculty occurrence

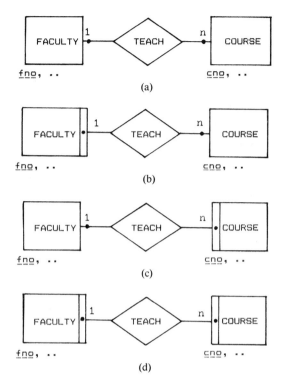

Figure 6.6   The ER type diagrams related to the ER occurrence diagrams in Figure 6.5.

(giving the m), and each faculty occurrence can be tied to more than one course occurrence (giving the n).

6.3 A COMMENT ON GRAPHICAL NOTATION

There is no single, universally accepted, form for the graphical notation used with the ER method. Although the methods given by various authors are similar in nature, they do differ from one another in both small and large ways. The graphical notation and terminology presented here follows that proposed by Howe.[1] A fairly standard notation is used by Ullman,[2]

[1]D. R. Howe, *Data Analysis for Database Design* (Baltimore, MD: Edward Arnold/ University Park Press, 1983).

[2]J. D. Ullman, *Principles of Database Systems,* 2nd edition, (Rockville, MD: Computer Science Press, 1984).

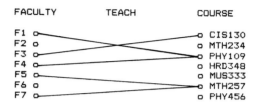

(a) Degree n:1 with neither entity's membership obligatory

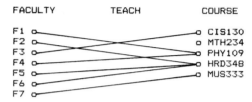

(b) Degree n:1 with the FACULTY entity's membership obligatory

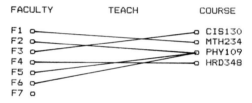

(c) Degree n:1 with the COURSE entity's membership obligatory

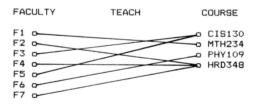

(d) Degree n:1 with both entity's membership obligatory

Figure 6.7 Examples of ER occurrence diagrams when the degree of the relationship is n:1.

while a more complex approach, using semantic nets, is presented by Hawryszkiewycz.[3] The reader is urged to review other methods, and to use the one that suits him or her best. It is felt that the method given here is straightforward and easy to use.

[3] I. T. Hawryszkiewycz, *Data Analysis and Design* (Chicago: Science Research Associates, Inc., 1984).

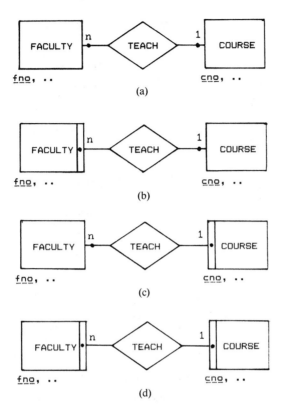

Figure 6.8   The ER type diagrams related to the ER occurrence diagrams in Figure 6.7.

6.4 PROBLEMS FOR CHAPTER 6

1. Draw typical entity occurrence diagrams for each of the following situations. List the assumptions being made in each case:

   a) A grocery chain wishes to store information on individual stores and the suppliers from whom each store buys produce. Each store buys produce from several suppliers and each supplier furnishes produce for several stores.

   b) A house painting service wishes to keep track of union painters and the house that each painter is currently painting. Each painter paints only one house at a time, but several painters can be painting on one house. Some painters may be unemployed. Only houses that are being painted are to be considered.

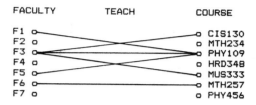

(a) Degree m:n with neither entity's membership obligatory

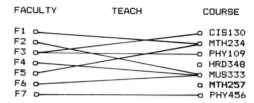

(b) Degree m:n with the FACULTY entity's membership obligatory

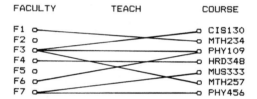

(c) Degree m:n with the COURSE entity's membership obligatory

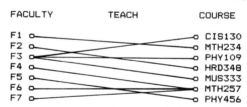

(d) Degree m:n with both entity's membership obligatory

Figure 6.9 Examples of ER occurrence diagrams when the degree of the relationship is m:n.

   c) A garage has mechanics working on automobiles. Each mechanic works on several autos, but each auto is worked on by only one mechanic.

2. Draw the ER type diagrams for each occurrence diagram from Problem 1. Note the entity keys in each figure.

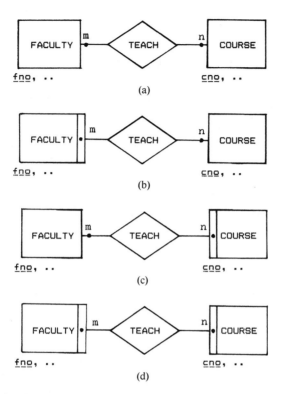

Figure 6.10   The ER type diagrams related to the ER occurrence diagrams in Figure 6.9.

7

DEVELOPING RELATIONS FROM THE ER TYPE DIAGRAM

Because it relates only two entities, the TEACH relationship that exists between FACULTY and COURSE (the two entities that were discussed in the last chapter) is called a **binary relationship.** Higher order relationships relating three or more entities will be discussed in the next chapter. Binary relationships are the most common. This chapter will be dedicated to showing how the relations for a database can be developed using ER type diagrams, in those cases where binary relationships are present.

The general approach to developing a database using the ER method is to first draw an ER type diagram which includes all of the entities and relationships that are important to the enterprise. As a specific example, Figure 7.1 gives one version of the complete ER diagram for the Bowling Secretary's Database. This diagram has four entities and three binary relationships. The second step in the design process is to deduce a set of "preliminary" design relations, along with a proposed primary key for each relation. The last step is to develop a list of all attributes of interest (which haven't already been listed as entity keys in the ER type diagram) and assign each of these attributes to one of the preliminary relations in such a way that BCNF relations result. In this last step, the FD's that exist between the attributes in each relation must be determined in order to check for BCNF.

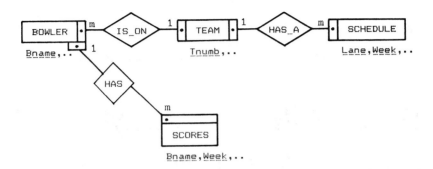

Other attributes: Phone, Stret, Stavg, Tname,
                     Captn, Game1, Game2, Game3

Figure 7.1   An ER type diagram for a bowling secretary's database.

If the relations so developed are not BCNF, or if there seems to be no logical preliminary relation in which to place some of the attributes, then the ER diagram must be revised to remove the troubles that are present.

7.1 PRELIMINARY RELATIONS FOR BINARY RELATIONSHIPS OF DEGREE 1:1

The preliminary relations that should be used for a given binary relationship can be deduced by looking at several logical alternatives, and then finding which of the alternatives is best. A set of general rules for generating relations from ER type diagrams can be developed using membership class and degree of the relationship as the determining factors. To help in developing these rules, the FACULTY TEACH COURSE situation (discussed at length in Chapter 6) will be used, along with liberal references to the diagrams displayed in Chapter 6. For the moment, discussion will be limited to those cases where the degree of the binary relationship is 1:1.

When trying to determine how many relations it will take to hold the information contained in binary relationships with degree 1:1 (like those shown in the ER type diagrams given in Figure 6.4), the simplest solution to hope for is that only one relation is needed. Assume that this one relation is called FACULTY, and that all the attributes are to be placed into this one relation. Figure 7.2 gives an instance of such a relation in the specific case where the membership class of both entities is obligatory (see Figures 6.3(d) and 6.4(d)). In this relation, two typical attributes have been added to the FACULTY entity: faculty_name (fname) and faculty_phone

FACULTY(<u>fno</u>, fname, fphone, cno, preq)

FACULTY

fno	fname	fphone	cno	preq
F1	Smith	2345	HRD348	HRD100
F2	Jones	2233	PHY109	NONE
F3	Hoppe	6543	CIS130	MTH120
F4	Apple	7766	MTH234	MTH150

Figure 7.2   Instance of a single relation holding the data from Figures 6.3(d) and 6.4(d).

(fphone). One attribute has been added to the COURSE entity: prerequisite (preq).

In this specific case, one relation is all that is needed. Since the degree of the relationship here is 1:1, and the membership class is obligatory for both FACULTY and COURSE, it is guaranteed that each fno value and each cno value will appear in any instance only once. This means that the relation will never be forced to hold any null data, or any repeated groups of redundant data. The entity key from FACULTY was chosen as the primary key for the relation, but the entity key from COURSE could have been used.

The first relation generation rule can now be stated:

RULE 1:   When the degree of a binary relationship is 1:1 with the membership class of both entities obligatory, only one relation is required. The primary key of this relation can be the entity key from either entity.

If the degree of the relationship is 1:1 and the membership class of one entity is obligatory, but the other is nonobligatory, one relation will not be sufficient to hold the data. Figure 7.3 gives an instance of the case where the membership class of FACULTY is obligatory and COURSE is non-

FACULTY(fno, fname, fphone, cno, preq)

FACULTY

fno	fname	fphone	cno	preq
F1	Smith	2345	HRD348	HRD100
F2	Jones	2233	PHY109	NONE
F3	Hoppe	6543	CIS130	MTH120
--	-----	----	MTH234	MTH150

Figure 7.3   Instance of a single relation holding the data from Figures 6.3(b) and 6.4(b).

obligatory (see Figures 6.3(b) and 6.4(b)). In this relation, nulls appear in all tuples that hold information on courses that aren't being taught by any faculty member. The nulls are symbolized with $--$'s.

After some thought, it can be deduced that the way to remove the null data is to use two relations rather than one. Each relation will hold the information from one entity. Additionally, the entity key from the non-obligatory side must be placed as an attribute in the relation holding information from the obligatory side. This case is shown in Figure 7.4. The reason that there are no nulls in the FACULTY relation in Figure 7.4 is that it has been assumed that every faculty member must teach exactly one course. (Note that if a faculty member could teach more than one course, there would be repeated values appearing in the fname and fphone fields for all faculty who are teaching more than one course.) It is important to emphasize that the word NONE, which appears as a value in the preq field in Figure 7.4, is a true value, not a null value.

The second relation generation rule can now be stated:

RULE 2:   When the degree of a binary relationship is 1:1 with the membership class of one entity obligatory, and the other nonobligatory, two relations are required. There must be one relation for each entity, with the entity key serving as the primary key for the corresponding relation. Additionally, the entity key from the nonobligatory side must be added as an attribute in the relation on the obligatory side.

Using this rule, the relations for the situation contained in Figures 6.3(c) and 6.4(c), where the membership class of COURSE is obligatory, but FACULTY is not, are

FACULTY(<u>fno</u>, fname, fphone)
COURSE(<u>cno</u>, preq, fno)

FACULTY(<u>fno</u>, fname, fphone, cno)
COURSE(<u>cno</u>, preq)

FACULTY

fno	fname	fphone	cno
F1	Smith	2345	HRD348
F2	Jones	2233	PHY109
F3	Hoppe	6543	CIS130

COURSE

cno	preq
CIS130	MTH120
HRD348	HRD100
MTH234	MTH150
PHY109	NONE

Figure 7.4   Instances of two relations holding the data related to Figures 6.3(b) and 6.4(b).

In the case where the degree of the binary relationship is 1:1 and the membership class of neither entity is obligatory, one relation is not sufficient. If only one relation were used, null values would appear in two different ways. Also, two relations aren't sufficient, because the mapping of the entity key from one entity into the opposite side's relation causes problems. The only solution is to use three relations: one for each entity, and one for the relationship. Figure 7.5 gives typical instances resulting from the use of one, two, and three relations in such a case (see Figures 6.3(a) and 6.4(a)). Here nulls appear in all but the case where three relations are used.

In the relation TEACH in Figure 7.5(c), any faculty_number value and any course_number value can appear only once, since the degree is 1:1. Also, TEACH holds only course_numbers for those courses that are being taught, and only faculty_numbers for those faculty who are teaching a course. The FACULTY relation holds information on all faculty members, and the COURSE relation holds information on all courses.

FACULTY

fno	fname	fphone	cno	preq
F1	Smith	2345	HRD348	HRD100
F2	Jones	2233	------	------
F3	Hoppe	6543	CIS130	MTH120
F4	Apple	7766	PHY109	NONE
--	-----	----	MTH234	MTH150

(a) Using one relation

FACULTY

fno	fname	fphone	cno
F1	Smith	2345	HRD348
F2	Jones	2233	------
F3	Hoppe	6543	CIS130
F4	Apple	7766	PHY109

COURSE

cno	preq	fno
CIS130	MTH120	F3
HRD348	HRD100	F1
MTH234	MTH150	--
PHY109	NONE	F4

(b) Using two relations

FACULTY

fno	fname	fphone
F1	Smith	2345
F2	Jones	2233
F3	Hoppe	6543
F4	Apple	7766

COURSE

cno	preq
CIS130	MTH120
HRD348	HRD100
MTH234	MTH150
PHY109	NONE

TEACH

fno	cno
F1	HRD348
F3	CIS130
F4	PHY109

(c) Using three relations

Figure 7.5 Possible relational forms for the binary relationship case with degree 1:1 and neither entity's membership class obligatory.

The third relation generation rule can now be stated:

RULE 3:   When the degree of a binary relationship is 1:1 with the membership class of neither entity obligatory, three relations are required: one for each entity, with the entity key serving as the primary key for the corresponding relation, and one for the relationship. The relationship will have among its attributes the entity keys from each entity.

In the case under discussion, the relation TEACH, which was generated from the relationship, had no attributes assigned other than those needed for the key. This is not always the case. For instance, if each course that was being taught had a student tutor assigned, the tutor's name could be an attribute that would appear in the TEACH relation.

7.2 EXAMPLE ER PROBLEM NUMBER ONE

Problem Definition

A database is to be designed to hold information on Northern Minnesota professional fishing guides and the lakes in which they operate. The International Fishing Guide's Union permits a maximum of one professional guide per lake and, by a gentleman's agreement among the guides, each guide operates in only one lake. Attributes of interest are the guide's name (gname), phone number (phone), daily fee (fee) and the maximum number of people allowed in a fishing party (size), the lake's name (lname), fishing rating (ratng), and the main type of fish caught in the lake (type).

Problem Solution

The entities here are GUIDE and LAKE with the relationship between them being OPERATE_IN. Typical ER occurrence and type diagrams are given in Figure 7.6. The assumptions made in these diagrams are that all guides are working, guide names are unique, lake names are unique, and that some lakes of interest don't have professional guides assigned to them.

Since the degree of the relationship is 1:1, with the membership class of one entity obligatory while the other is nonobligatory, RULE 2 is used to generate the preliminary relations:

> GUIDE(gname,............,lname)
> LAKE(lname,....)

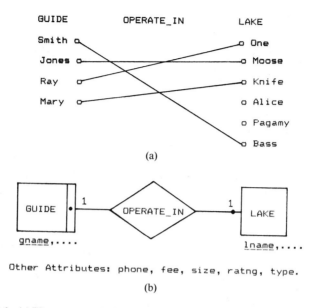

Figure 7.6   (a) ER occurrence and (b) type diagrams for Example ER Problem One.

There is no problem in finding a "home" for those attributes not used as entity keys: phone, size, and fee go into the GUIDE relation, since they contain guide information; and ratng and type go into the LAKE relation, since they hold information about lakes. The proposed design relations are thus:

GUIDE(gname, phone, size, fee, name)
LAKE(name, ratng, type)

Figure 7.7 gives the FD diagram for each relation, which shows that each relation is in BCNF. Figure 7.8 gives typical instances of the relations used for the database. See page 80.

This same database will be analyzed with different assumptions later in this chapter.

7.3 PRELIMINARY RELATIONS FOR BINARY RELATIONSHIPS OF DEGREE 1:N

In those situations where the degree of a binary relationship is 1:1, it takes three separate rules to determine the generation of an appropriate set of preliminary relations. When the degree of the binary relationship is 1:n,

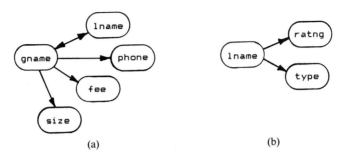

Figure 7.7   FD diagrams for the (a) GUIDE and (b) LAKE relations in Example ER Problem One.

GUIDE

gname	phone	fee	size	lname
Jones	234-6789	50	4	Moose
Mary	234-8765	45	3	Knife
Ray	234-8765	55	4	One
Smith	234-7766	55	4	Bass

LAKE

lname	ratng	type
Alice	good	bass
Bass	excel	walleye
Moose	avg	n_pike
Knife	poor	n_pike
One	good	perch
Pagamy	avg	sm_bass

Figure 7.8   Typical instances of the GUIDE and LAKE relations.

only two rules are required. The feature that determines which of the two rules to use is the membership class of the n-side: the membership class of the 1-side does not affect the end result in either case.

Figure 7.9(b) is an instance of a single relation, COURSE, that holds the data from Figures 6.5(c) and 6.6(c). The type diagram from Figure 6.6(c) has been repeated here for clarity. This is a case where the degree is 1:n with the membership class of the n-side obligatory and the 1-side nonobligatory. There are two distinct problems with this relation. Nulls appear in those course attribute fields where the faculty member is not teaching a class; there are repeated fields of faculty data in those cases where a faculty member teaches more than one class. (Specifically, the information on faculty member F5 appears three times.) If the 1-side were obligatory, rather than nonobligatory, the nulls would disappear, but the repeated groups of data in the faculty attribute fields would remain.

To solve all of these problems, regardless of the membership class of the 1-side, the following rule can be followed:

RULE 4:   When the degree of a binary relationship is 1:n with the membership class of the n-side obligatory, two relations are required: one

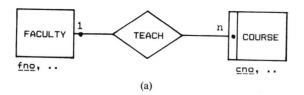

(a)

COURSE

cno	preq	fno	fname	fphone
CIS130	MTH120	F3	Hoppe	6543
MTH234	MTH150	F1	Smith	2345
PHY109	NONE	F2	Jones	2233
HRD348	HRD100	F5	Scott	4356
MUS333	MUS100	F5	Scott	4356
MTH257	MTH234	F5	Scott	4356
PHY456	PHY109	F7	Poppy	8122
-------	--------	F4	Apple	7766
-------	--------	F6	Caine	5492

(b)

Figure 7.9   Using one relation for 1:n binary relationship with the membership class of the n-side obligatory and the 1-side nonobligatory.

for each entity, with the entity key from each entity serving as the primary key for the corresponding relation. Additionally, the entity key from the 1-side must be added as an attribute in the relation on the n-side.

Figure 7.10 gives instances of the two relations developed using this rule and holding the same information as is contained in Figure 7.9. Notice that all nulls and repeating groups of data have been eliminated.

Figure 7.11(b) is an instance of a single relation, COURSE, that holds the data from Figures 6.5(a) and 6.6(a). The type diagram from Figure 6.6(a) has been repeated here for clarity. This is a case where the degree is 1:n with the membership class of both sides nonobligatory. There are three distinct problems with this relation. Nulls appear in course attribute fields

COURSE

cno	preq	fno
CIS130	MTH120	F3
MTH234	MTH150	F1
PHY109	NONE	F2
HRD348	HRD100	F5
MUS333	MUS100	F5
MTH257	MTH234	F5
PHY456	PHY109	F7

FACULTY

fno	fname	fphone
F1	Smith	2345
F2	Jones	2233
F3	Hoppe	6543
F4	Apple	7766
F5	Scott	4356
F6	Caine	5492
F7	Poppy	8122

Figure 7.10   Data from Figure 7.9 placed into two relations using RULE 4.

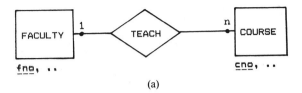

(a)

COURSE

cno	preq	fno	fname	fphone
CIS130	MTH120	F3	Hoppe	6543
MTH234	MTH150	F2	Jones	2233
PHY109	NONE	F2	Jones	2233
HRD348	HRD100	F5	Scott	4356
MUS333	MUS100	--	-----	----
MTH257	MTH234	F5	Scott	4356
PHY456	PHY109	F5	Scott	4356
------	------	F1	Smith	2345
------	------	F4	Apple	7766
------	------	F6	Poppy	8122

(b)

Figure 7.11   Using one relation for 1:n binary relationship with the membership class of both sides nonobligatory.

where the faculty member is not teaching a class, and in those faculty attribute fields where the course is not being taught by any faculty member. Additionally, there are repeated fields of faculty data in those cases where a faculty member teaches more than one class. (Specifically, the information on faculty member F2 appears twice, and the information on faculty member F5 appears three times.) If the 1-side were obligatory, rather than nonobligatory, the nulls in the course attribute fields would disappear, but the nulls and repeated groups of data in the faculty attribute fields would remain.

If RULE 4 is applied in this case, generating two relations similar to those in Figure 7.10, all the problems would disappear except one: there would still be nulls in faculty_number fields in the new COURSE relation in all those places where a course is not being taught. An instance showing this is in Figure 7.12.

To solve all of these problems, regardless of the membership class of the 1-side, the following rule can be followed:

RULE 5:   When the degree of a binary relationship is 1:n with the membership class of the n-side nonobligatory, three relations are required: one for each entity, with the entity key from each entity serving as the primary key for the corresponding relation, and one for the relationship. The relationship will have among its attributes the entity keys from each entity.

Figure 7.13 gives instances of the three relations developed using this

COURSE

cno	preq	fno
CIS130	MTH120	F3
MTH234	MTH150	F2
PHY109	NONE	F2
HRD348	HRD100	F5
MUS333	MUS100	--
MTH257	MTH234	F5
PHY456	PHY109	F5

FACULTY

fno	fname	fphone
F1	Smith	2345
F2	Jones	2233
F3	Hoppe	6543
F4	Apple	7766
F5	Scott	4356
F6	Caine	5492
F7	Poppy	8122

Figure 7.12   Data from Figure 7.11 placed into two relations using RULE 4.

COURSE

cno	preq
CIS130	MTH120
MTH234	MTH150
PHY109	NONE
HRD348	HRD100
MUS333	MUS100
MTH257	MTH234
PHY456	PHY109

FACULTY

fno	fname	fphone
F1	Smith	2345
F2	Jones	2233
F3	Hoppe	6543
F4	Apple	7766
F5	Scott	4356
F6	Caine	5492
F7	Poppy	8122

TEACH

fno	cno
F2	MTH234
F2	PHY109
F3	CIS130
F5	HRD348
F5	MTH257
F5	PHY456

cno is the primary
key due to the n:1
relationship between
cno and fno.

Figure 7.13   Data from Figure 7.11 placed into three relations using RULE 5.

rule that hold the same information contained in Figure 7.11. Notice that all nulls and repeating groups of data have been eliminated.

7.4 PRELIMINARY RELATIONS FOR BINARY RELATIONSHIPS OF DEGREE M:N

When the degree of a binary relationship is m:n, three relations are required to store the data, regardless of the membership class of either entity. If one or two relations are used, nulls and/or repeating groups of data will appear in instances of the relations: which of the two problems arises, when only two relations are used, is dependent upon the membership classes of the two entities. The rule to follow in generating preliminary relations for the m:n case is

RULE 6:   When the degree of a binary relationship is m:n, three relations are required: one for each entity, with the entity key from each entity serving as the primary key for the corresponding relation, and one for the relationship. The relation from the relationship will have among its attributes the entity keys from each entity.

Figure 7.14 gives instances of the relations containing the data given in Figure 6.9(a) (degree of m:n with neither membership class obligatory). Note that no nulls, or repeating groups of data, are present in any instance. Instances of the relations holding the same data when one (or both) memberships' class is obligatory would be similar. The reader should draw instances of two relations holding these same data, to illustrate the reasons why three relations are required.

7.5 EXAMPLE ER PROBLEM NUMBER TWO

Problem Definition

This is an expansion of the fishing guide problem defined in Section 7.2. A database is to be designed to hold information on Northern Min-

COURSE

cno	preq
CIS130	MTH120
MTH234	MTH150
PHY109	NONE
HRD348	HRD100
MUS333	MUS100
MTH257	MTH234
PHY456	PHY109

FACULTY

fno	fname	fphone
F1	Smith	2345
F2	Jones	2233
F3	Hoppe	6543
F4	Apple	7766
F5	Scott	4356
F6	Caine	5492
F7	Poppy	8122

TEACH

fno	cno
F1	PHY109
F3	CIS130
F3	PHY109
F3	MUS133
F5	PHY109
F6	MTH257

This relation is "all key".[1]

Figure 7.14   Data from Figure 6.9(a) placed into three relations using RULE 6.

[1]When there are no FDs relating any of the attributes in a relation, the primary key for that relation requires the use of all of the attributes. The primary key for TEACH would be >fno,cno<. Relations of this type are said to be "all key." All key relations are in Boyce Codd Normal Form.

nesota professional fishing guides and the lakes in which they operate. The International Fishing Guide's Union permits several professional guides to operate in the same lake, but, by a gentleman's agreement among the guides, each guide operates in only one lake. Fishermen who hire the guides are interested in what types of fish are available in each lake, the biggest fish of each type caught in the region this season, and the type of bait that is considered by the union as the best bait for each type of fish in the region. Attributes of interest are the guide's name (gname), phone number (phone), daily fee (fee), name of the lake in which the guide operates (lname) and the maximum number of people allowed in a fishing party (size), the fishing rating of each lake (ratng) and the main types of fish caught in each lake (type), the weight of the largest fish of each type caught in the region this season (wbig), and the best bait for each type of fish (bait).

Problem Solution

The entities of interest are GUIDE, LAKE, and FISH, with the relationships OPERATE_IN and HAS, as shown in Figure 7.15, where the type diagram and a typical occurrence diagram are given. Two relationships

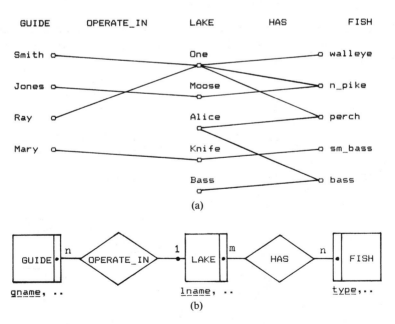

Figure 7.15   (a) ER occurrence and (b) ER type diagrams for Example ER Problem Number Two.

are present; one is n:1 and the other is m:n. Both RULES 4 and 6 must be applied, and four preliminary relations will result: one preliminary relation for each entity, and one for the relationship HAS. Additionally, the lname attribute from LAKE must be added to the relation for GUIDE (from RULE 4). The resulting preliminary relations are

GUIDE(<u>gname</u>, ...,lname)
LAKE(<u>lname</u>, ...)
LK_FSH(<u>lname, type</u>,.....)
FISH(<u>type</u>,.....)

where the preliminary relation from HAS has been named LK_FSH. As was the case in Example ER Problem Number One, there is no problem in placing those attributes that are not part of an entity key into the preliminary relations to form the final relations: phone, fee, and size are all properties of entity GUIDE and go in that relation. ratng is a property of LAKE, while bait and wbig all are related to FISH. The only preliminary relation that gets no additional attributes is LK_FSH, which turns out to be all key.

GUIDE(<u>gname</u>,phone,fee,size,lname)
LAKE(<u>lname</u>,ratng)
LK_FSH(<u>lname, type</u>)
FISH(<u>type</u>,wbig,bait)

Figure 7.16 gives the FD diagram for each of the relations. Each is already in BCNF, so no further reductions are required. Typical instances of each relation are given in Figure 7.17.

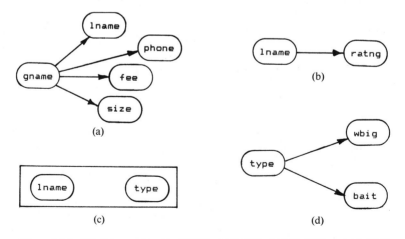

Figure 7.16 FD diagrams for (a) GUIDE, (b) LAKE, (c) LK_FSH and (d) FISH relations for Figure 7.15.

GUIDE

gname	phone	fee	size	lname
Jones	234-6789	50	4	Moose
Mary	234-8765	45	3	Knife
Ray	234-8765	55	4	One
Smith	234-7766	55	4	Bass

LAKE

lname	ratng
Alice	good
Bass	excel
Moose	avg
Knife	poor
One	good

LK_FSH

lname	type
One	walleye
One	n_pike
One	perch
Moose	n_pike
Knife	n_pike
Alice	bass
Alice	perch
Bass	bass
Knife	sm_bass

FISH

type	wbig	bait
bass	6.5	pls_worm
n_pike	27.5	spoon
perch	0.75	worm
sm_bass	4.25	leech
walleye	12.8	crawler

Figure 7.17   Typical instances of the relations discussed in Example ER Problem Number Two.

The reader is urged to determine the ramifications of each of the following changes to the solution of the problem just discussed:

1. Guides can operate in several lakes;
2. The desire is to store information on all baits that work for a given fish type, not just the "best" one.

7.6 THE BOWLING SECRETARY'S DATABASE REVISITED

Figure 7.18 gives a first attempt at an ER type diagram for the bowling secretary's database discussed in detail in Chapter 5. Three entities and two binary relationships are assumed to be sufficient to model the information.

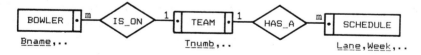

Other attributes: Phone, Stret, Stavg, Tname,
                    Captn, Game1, Game2, Game3

Figure 7.18   A possible ER type diagram for the bowling secretary's database.

Using this diagram, and the rules for generating relations discussed earlier in this chapter, three preliminary relations can be developed. The entities BOWLER, TEAM, and SCHEDULE each generate one relation. Additionally, the entity key (Tnumb) from TEAM must be placed as an attribute in the other two relations, because of the 1:n relationships that exist between TEAM and the other entities. The three preliminary relations are

> BOWLER(Bname, ..., Tnumb)
> TEAM(Tnumb, ...)
> SCHEDULE(Lane, Week, Tnumb)

Logical places to assign the other attributes, listed in Figure 7.18, are as follows: Tname and Captn should go into TEAM, since these attributes are the team name and team captain; Phone, Stret, and Stavg go into BOWLER, since they hold information on the bowlers. There is no good place to put Game1, Game2, and Game3. At first glance, it would appear that they should also go into BOWLER, but game scores lose some meaning when it is not known in which week the games were bowled. However, Week can't be added to BOWLER, since it doesn't appear in the list of unassigned attributes. This situation indicates that there must be an error in the ER type diagram. It is possible that an alteration of the ER type diagram would result in preliminary relations that do yield BCNF relations directly. The ER type diagram given in Figure 7.1 is such a diagram. It was developed using the results of the previous discussions as a guide. The new entity here is SCORES, and has as the entity key the composite ⟨Bname, Week⟩.

The preliminary relations developed from Figure 7.1 are

> BOWLER(Bname, ... , Tnumb)
> TEAM(Tnumb, ...)
> SCHEDULE(Lane, Week, Tnumb)
> SCORES(Bname, Week, ... , Bname).

An interesting point has arisen in the preliminary relation SCORES: Bname appears twice; once since it is part of the entity key for SCORES, and once due to placement of the entity key from BOWLER into SCORES, as dictated by the 1:n relationship between the entities BOWLER and SCORES. This happens occasionally when a composite entity key is present on the n-side of a 1:n relationship. All that needs to be done in this case is to drop one of the two duplicate attributes, to avoid redundancy. An arrow has been placed through the last Bname to indicate that it should be eliminated.

When the remaining attributes are added to the last set of preliminary relations, the same four BCNF relations developed in Chapter 5 are generated. This example illustrates the fact that the ER type diagram may be evolved through a process of iteration.

7.7 A COMMENT ON THE NUMBER OF RELATIONS

The general rules given in this chapter for the generation of preliminary relations for a given ER diagram differ somewhat from some presentations found in the literature. Some authors state that one preliminary relation should be developed for each entity and one for each relationship, regardless of degree and membership class. In most cases this method will generate more relations than are needed.

7.8 PROBLEMS FOR CHAPTER 7

1. Develop the relations for each type diagram from Problem 2 in Chapter 6.

2. Redraw the BOWLER HAS SCORES section of the ER diagram in Figure 7.1 with the assumption that the entity key for the SCORES entity is

   (a) ⟨Week,Game1,Game2,Game3⟩

   and

   (b) ⟨Game1,Game2,Game3⟩

Draw a typical occurrence diagram in each case. Generate the preliminary relations and discuss the problems related to the assignment of the other attributes.

8

ADDITIONAL
ER METHOD CONSTRUCTS

In Chapters 6 and 7, a method for generating database relations using binary relationships was developed. Although many real-world situations can be characterized using only binary relationships, situations will arise in which a reasonable model of the enterprise cannot be obtained without the use of additional constructs. This chapter will introduce two new ER method constructs: higher-order relationships and roles.

8.1 THE NEED FOR HIGHER ORDER RELATIONSHIPS

In Chapter 7, two example problems were investigated using the ER method. Both examples were based on the need to store information on fishing guides, the lakes in which the guides operated, and the types of fish present in the lakes. Assume for the moment that people who hire a guide would like to know the main type of fish for which a guide would prefer to fish. Looking at the occurrence diagram in Figure 7.15(a), one might be tempted to deduce that since Smith operates in Lake One, and since Lake One has walleye, northern pike, and perch, it follows that Smith likes to fish for walleye, northern pike, and perch. This may or may not be true. It could be that Smith only guides for people who wish to fish for walleye. If a relationship between GUIDE and FISH exists, this relationship, call it PRE-FERS, should be shown in both the type and the occurrence diagrams, as in Figure 8.1. In this figure, dashed lines have been used for the PREFERS relationship occurrences, to make them more visible. In addition, in order to avoid confusion, only a few occurrences have been shown.

The occurrence diagram shows that Smith operates in Lake One, Lake One holds three types of fish, and Smith prefers to fish for walleye. Due to the fact that the degree of the relationship between GUIDE and FISH is n:1, and since each guide fishes in one lake, there is no confusion over which guides you would use in a given lake if you wanted to fish for a given type of fish. In fact, if you generate the relations that should be used for the situation given in Figure 8.1, you will find that the only change required in the relations shown in Figure 7.17 is that the attribute type from FISH has to be added to relation GUIDE. (This attribute indicates the fish-type preferred by a given guide.) Thus, in this expanded example, binary relationships still give a correct model of the situation.

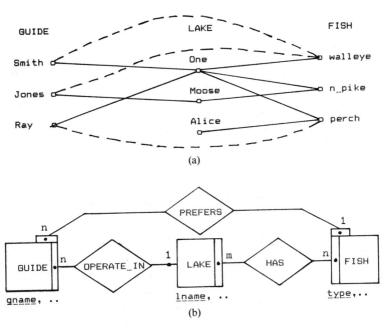

Figure 8.1 (a) ER occurrence and (b) ER type diagrams when guides have a fish preference.

If the problem is further modified, however, it can be shown that binary relationships will not correctly model the situation. Assume now that guides operate in more than one lake, and that a guide might prefer to fish for one type of fish in one lake, but a different type of fish in another lake. Smith, for instance, prefers to fish for walleye in Lake One, but for northern pike in Moose Lake. Jones, as a second example, might operate only in Moose Lake and prefers to fish for northern pike. Grouping these pieces of data together, it can be stated that

> Smith operates in both Lake One and Moose Lake.
>
> Jones operates only in Moose Lake.
>
> Smith prefers walleye in Lake One.
>
> Smith prefers n_pike in Moose Lake.
>
> Jones prefers n_pike in Moose Lake.

The ER occurrence diagram, using binary relationships that include only these five pieces of data, is shown in Figure 8.2. The important item to note here is that, although the information stated above on Smith and Jones can be deduced from the diagram, it can also be deduced that Smith prefers

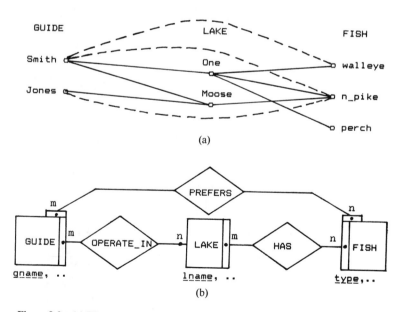

Figure 8.2   (a) ER occurrence and (b) type diagrams with all relationships of degree m:n.

n_pike in Lake One, which is not true! The problem here stems from the fact that all the relationships have a degree of m:n, which means there is no way of storing a unique path that connects all three entity occurrences together in a unique manner. A clue to the fact that such a problem exists is found by noting that each of the statements, "Smith prefers walleye in Lake One" and "Smith prefers n_pike in Moose Lake" ties three pieces of information together. The same information can't be preserved by saying: "Smith guides in Lake One and in Moose Lake"; "Lake One and Moose Lake have walleye, northern pike, and perch"; and "Smith prefers to fish for walleye and northern pike." The situation is such that triplets of information can't be modeled as a set of three binary relationships. A correct modeling is given in Figure 8.3 and requires a three-way relationship.

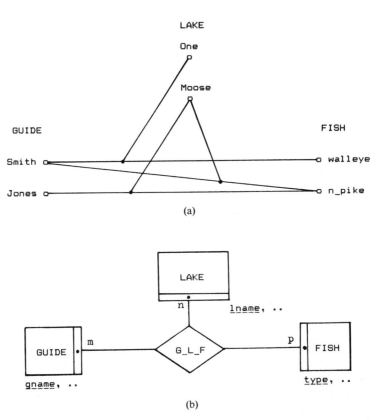

Figure 8.3 (a) ER occurrence and (b) ER type diagrams for a three-way relationship G_L_F.

8.2 PRELIMINARY RELATIONS
FOR THREE-WAY RELATIONSHIPS

When three-way relationships are encountered, the preliminary relations are generated using the following rule:

RULE 7:   When a relationship is three-way, four preliminary relations are required: one for each entity, with the entity key from each entity serving as the primary key for the corresponding relation; and one for the relationship. The relation generated by the relationship will have among its attributes the entity keys from each entity. (Similarly, when a relationship is n-way, $n+1$ preliminary relations are required.)

Using this rule with the data in Figure 8.3, the preliminary relations are

> GUIDE(gname,......)
> LAKE(lname,.......)
> FISH(type,........)
> G_L_F(gname,lname,type,...)

The primary key for G_L_F can't be determined until all of the "other" attributes have been assigned. If all of the attributes given in Figure 7.17 are retained, the GUIDE relation would be assigned the following attributes: phone, fee, and size; the LAKE relation would be assigned only one attribute, ratng; and the FISH relation would be assigned wbig and bait. The G_L_F relation would get no other attributes. The primary key for G_L_F would be the composite ⟨gname,lname⟩, if each guide had only one preferred fish in a lake. If the guide had two or more preferred fish in any one lake, then G_L_F would be "all key." Figure 8.4 (p. 96) gives instances of the four relations under the assumption that each guide has one preferred type of fish in each lake in which the guide operates. Each of these relations can be shown to be in BCNF.

8.3 THE USE OF ROLES

Situations can arise in which entities and relationships alone are not sufficient to model an enterprise in a satisfactory manner. One such situation occurs when occurrences from the same entity must assume different roles in the business of the enterprise. As an example, assume that a small automotive supplier wishes to store information on manufacturing personnel.

GUIDE

gname	phone	fee	size
Jones	234-6789	50	4
Mary	234-8765	45	3
Ray	234-8765	55	4
Smith	234-7766	55	4

LAKE

lname	ratng
Alice	good
Moose	avg
Knife	poor
One	good

G_L_F

gname	lname	type
Jones	Moose	n_pike
Smith	Moose	n_pike
Smith	One	walleye
Ray	One	perch
Ray	Moose	n_pike
Mary	Knife	sm_bass

FISH

type	wbig	bait
bass	6.5	pls_worm
n_pike	27.5	spoon
perch	0.75	worm
sm_bass	4.25	leech
walleye	12.8	crawler

Figure 8.4 Instances of the relations generated from Figure 8.3.

There are two classes of employees: supervisors and assemblers. Supervisors are salaried, while assemblers are paid an hourly wage.

A first attempt at an ER diagram for the enterprise is given in Figure 8.5. The entity key for each entity is the social security number for the individual. It is assumed that no supervisor supervises another supervisor, no supervisor is an assembler, and no assembler is supervisor.

Since the relationship SUPERVISES is 1:n with both sides obligatory, the general rule is that two preliminary relations are required:

$$SUPER(supSS\#,.........................)$$
$$ASSEM(\overline{assmSS\#},.................,supSS\#)$$

One problem with this model is found when the nonkey attributes are added to the preliminary relations. Assume that the other attributes of interest are

ename — Name of an employee.

wphone — Work phone number for a supervisor. Assemblers do not have work phones.

Figure 8.5 Possible ER model for the enterprise.

hphone — Home phone number for an employee.

haddr — Home address for an employee.

hrate — Hourly rate of pay for an assembler.

salary — Monthly salary for a supervisor.

jcode — Job code for an assembler.

area — Area of expertise for a supervisor.

There is no problem in finding a home in one of the two relations for the following attributes: wphone, hrate, salary, jcode, and area. When each of these attributes is placed into a logical location in one of the two relations, the preliminary relations take on the form:

SUPER(supSS#,salary,area,wphone,.....)
ASSEM(assmSS#,hrate,jcode,......,supSS#)

The only attributes remaining are ename, hphone, and haddr. For completeness, these three attributes need to go into both relations. However, the general rule is to place each of the nonkey attributes into only one relation.

One might be tempted to redefine the three remaining attributes into the following six attributes:

sname — Name of a supervisor.

aname — Name of an assembler.

shphone — Home phone number for a supervisor.

shaddr — Home address for a supervisor.

ahphone — Home phone number for an assembler.

ahaddr — Home address for an assembler.

Sname, shphone, and shaddr could be placed into SUPER and aname, ahphone, and ahaddr could be placed into ASSEM. This is a poor solution, since it is merely a makeshift method of circumventing the problem of having no real home for the two original attributes.

If the proposed name changing of attributes were implemented, the following problem would arise. Suppose that it is required to find the home phone number for an employee, say, Joan Jones. Since it might not be known whether Joan Jones was a supervisor or an assembler, it would be necessary to search first one relation, and then the other, until the name Joan Jones was found. If it turned out that there were two Joan Joneses, one a supervisor and the other an assembler, a search of the wrong relation would give an incorrect phone number.

A better solution to the problem is obtained by viewing the overall problem from a different perspective. Supervisors and assemblers can all be viewed as employees, with supervisor and assembler being roles that a given employee can assume: some employees are supervisors, while other employees are assemblers. This can be depicted graphically as shown in Figure 8.6. In this figure, EMPLOYEE is an entity with employee social security number as the entity key. Objects from this entity (referred to by some as an entity set) can assume roles as either supervisors or assemblers. The two role-playing sets, SUPERVISOR and ASSEMBLER, are connected by the relationship SUPERVISES. The arrows that go from EMPLOYEE to both SUPERVISOR and ASSEMBLER indicate that EMPLOYEE is the source entity, while SUPERVISOR and ASSEMBLER are roles.

To generate preliminary relations from the diagram in Figure 8.6, the next rule can be followed:

The source entity will generate one relation, with the entity key serving as the key for the relation. The role-playing items and their associated relationships will generate the number of relations specified by the previous rules of thumb, where each role is treated like a regular entity.

The three preliminary relations generated using this rule are

EMPLOYEE(empSS#,.............)
SUPER(supSS#,................)
ASSEM(assmSS#, ...,supSS#)

When assignments of the other attributes are made into this set of relations, it is found that each attribute has a natural home. The final relations that result are

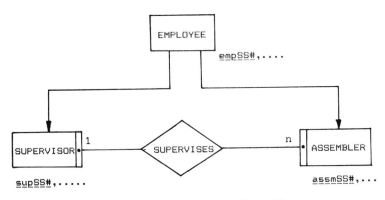

Figure 8.6 Use of roles in an ER model.

EMPLOYEE(empSS#,ename,hphone,haddr)
SUPER(supSS#,salary,area,wphone)
ASSEM(assmSS#,hrate,jcode,supSS#)

The relation obtained from the source entity (EMPLOYEE) holds information that is common to all employees. The relations generated from the roles hold information that is specific to the role being played. Each role-generated relation is connected to the source-generated relation by a common domain attribute—social security number in this example.

In reviewing the diagram in Figure 8.6, it should be noted that the SUPERVISES relationship connects two roles that are from the same source entity. This type of relationship is said to be **recursive.** It is recursive in the sense that, from the source entity point of view, employees are supervising employees. There is no reason why roles from one source entity cannot have a relationship with roles from different source entities. In this case, the relationship would not be recursive.

To increase the speed of access during queries, a designer might wish to consider the addition of an attribute to the EMPLOYEE relation that would indicate whether the employee was a supervisor or an assembler. This would avoid the need to search the SUPER and ASSEM relations to determine the job type of an individual, once the social security number for that individual was known. There are reasons both for and against such an addition.

8.4 A LARGER ER DESIGN PROBLEM

Problem Definition

A database is to be designed for the Topnotch Intercollegiate Athletic Conference (TIAC). The database will be used by members of the staff in the TIAC commissioner's office. The commissioner's office controls all league activities including such things as setting the schedule in all league sports; hiring officials for all league contests; checking on the eligibility of all league athletes; plus keeping a roster of all athletes, administrators, and coaches for all colleges in the league.

The commissioner has identified the following items as being of prime importance:

1. For each institution in the league:
    Official name of the college
    Size of the student body

All sports participated in by the institution
Logo
Name of the fieldhouse and its capacity
Name of the football field and its capacity
Name, address, home phone number, and work phone number for
each of the following people:

President of the college
Athletic Director (AD)
Sports Information Director (SID)
Faculty Athletic Representative (FAR)
Head coach for each sport

2. A roster of all league-approved officials including:
Name and social security number
Home address
Home phone number
Sport in which they officiate
Coaches' rating from the past year
Specific contests to which the official has been assigned for the
coming season.

3. A roster of all student athletes including:
Name and social security number
Home address
College address
College phone number
Current major
Grade point average
Hours toward graduation
Number of seasons of competition in each sport participated in
Date of first entry into the college
Number of credit hours currently being taken
Number of credit hours completed in the last two terms

4. The league schedule for the coming year including:
Home team for each contest
Away team for each contest
Date and time of each contest
Officials assigned
Sport in which contest will occur

5. Each sport in the league has a rules committee, and one head coach
is appointed by the league as the chairperson of that committee.

The following assumptions can be made: the schedule is for the coming year; head coaches coach only one sport; some colleges don't participate

in all league sports; some people share the same office phone; the league has both men's and women's sports.

The ER Diagram

The main problem in the development of an ER diagram is the determination of the entities to be used; there is no unique set of entities in most cases. In this problem it was decided that the entities of interest are COLLEGE, SPORT, STUDENT, OFFICIAL, and EMPLOYEE. The EMPLOYEE entity was to represent all employees from all colleges in the league that had any affiliation with the league. Additionally, HEAD COACH was deemed to be a role that an EMPLOYEE could assume, while COLLEGEs could assume roles as either a HOME TEAM, or an AWAY TEAM, when it came to sporting events. The final ER diagram is given in Figure 8.7. Note in particular the four-way relationship of SCHEDULE.

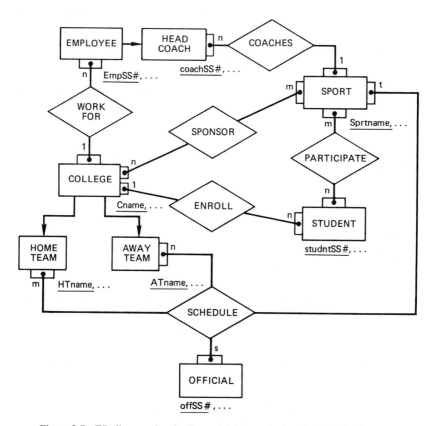

Figure 8.7   ER diagram for the Topnotch Intercollegiate Athletic Conference.

The Preliminary Relations

The preliminary relations that can be generated from Figure 8.7 are

```
COLLEGE(Cname,..........................)
EMPLOYEE(EmpSS#,.................,Cname)
HOME(HTname,..........................)
AWAY(ATname,..........................)
OFFICIAL(offSS#,......................)
COACH(coachSS#,...............,Sprtname)
SPORT(Sprtname,........................)
STUDENT(studntSS#,...............,Cname)
SPONSOR(Cname,Sprtname,................)
PARTIC(Sprtname,studntSS#,.............)
SCHED(HTname,ATname,offSS#,Sprtname,...)
```

When the other attributes are assigned, the following relations are obtained:

```
COLLEGE(Cname,fieldhouse_name,fieldhouse_capacity,
        football_field_name,football_field_capacity,
        enrollment)
EMPLOYEE(EmpSS#,emp_name,emp_addr,emp_hphone,emp_wphone,title,Cname)
HOME(HTname)
AWAY(ATname)
OFFICIAL(offSS#,off_name,off_addr, off_hphone,
         sport_in_which_approved)
COACH(coachSS#,Sprtname)
SPORT(Sprtname,SS#_of_rules_chairperson)
STUDENT(studntSS#,sex,age,gpa,total_credit_hours,
        studnt_address,Cname,credit_hours_this_term,
        credit_hours_last_two_terms)
SPONSOR(Cname,Sprtname)
PARTIC(Sprtname,studntSS#,seasons_of_competition)
SCHED(HTname,ATname,offSS#,Sprtname,date,time_of_contest)
```

Two relations can be dropped from the last set. HOME and AWAY are unary relations that hold no useful information. They hold no useful information, since no attributes have been presented which are unique to a home or away team, rather than the college as a whole. Dropping these two relations gives what could be termed the tentative design relations.

TENTATIVE DESIGN RELATIONS

```
COLLEGE(Cname,fieldhouse_name,fieldhouse_capacity,
        football_field_name,football_field_capacity,
        enrollment)
```

EMPLOYEE(EmpSS#,emp_name,emp_addr,emp_hphone,emp_wphone,title,Cname)
OFFICIAL(offSS#,off_name,off_addr, off_hphone,
                    sport_in_which_approved)
COACH(coachSS#,Sprtname)
SPORT(Sprtname,SS#_of_rules_chairperson)
STUDENT(studntSS#,sex,age,gpa,total_credit_hours,
            studnt_address,Cname,credit_hours_this_term,
            credit_hours_last_two_terms)
SPONSOR(Cname,Sprtname)
PARTIC(Sprtname,studntSS#,seasons_of_competition)
SCHED(HTname,ATname,offSS#,Sprtname,date,time_of_contest)

The SCHED relation is one relation in the tentative design set that is in need of modification. If instances of SCHED are drawn, it will be found to contain sets of repeated data, since more than one official will be assigned to each league contest. One way to eliminate this problem is to redraw that portion of the ER diagram that relates to officials. This should be done in such a manner that BCNF relations are the result. A second way to eliminate the problem is to decompose SCHED using functional dependencies. These solutions are left as an exercise at the end of the chapter. All the relations in the tentative design set must be checked for BCNF; this also is left as an exercise at the end of the chapter.

8.5 PROBLEMS FOR CHAPTER 8

1. The following problems deal with the last set of design relations given in the ER problem in Section 8.4.
   a) Draw an FD diagram for each relation and see if it is in BCNF. If a relation is not in BCNF try two solutions: (1) Redraw the ER diagram in such a way that BCNF relations are generated, and (2) decompose all non-BCNF relations into normal form.
   b) Draw instances of the final design relations and outline how they would be used to answer typical queries from the commissioner's office.
2. Discuss in detail how the following items would affect the ER diagram in Figure 8.7 and the final design relations:
   a) An official can officiate in more than one sport.
   b) A coach can be a head coach in more than one sport.
   c) Some colleges do not sponsor football and have no football field.
   d) Eliminate the binary relationships SPONSOR, ENROLL, and PARTICIPATE and replace them with one three-way relationship.
   e) Some sports, such as golf, do not use officials.

3. Draw an ER diagram and develop the relations for a database for a used car dealer. The dealer has a staff that consists of salespeople, secretaries, and mechanics. The salespeople are on a salary plus commission, while all other employees are hourly. Sales commissions are 5 percent for those salespeople with less than three years of service and 8 percent for those with three or more years of service. Information on autos in stock includes purchase date, assessed value, mechanical work to be done before selling, estimated cost of work to be done, auto make, model, model year, and basic color. Some mechanics have a specialty, such as engine overhaul or bump and dent. (Add any additional attributes that you feel are appropriate.)

9

IMPLEMENTING THE BOWLING SECRETARY'S DATABASE USING DBASE III

This chapter contains three main sections of information: (1) sample listings of the four relations that form the bowling secretary's database, as they were implemented in dBASE III; (2) examples of how dBASE III commands can be used with these relations to answer simple queries; and (3) an in-depth discussion of a set of menu-driven dBASE III program modules that answer complex queries using dBASE III commands embedded in the dBASE III programming language. The database implementation was developed on an IBM PC with 256K of memory, two double-sided disk drives, and a monochrome monitor. The dBASE III system disk is always in side A, and the program modules and database files are in side B.

9.1 THE CASE STUDY DATABASE IN DBASE III

Before proceeding with discussions of specific queries and various program modules, the actual database relations will be examined. The test data in the database were developed under the following assumptions:

1. The bowling league has six teams.
2. Each team has four bowlers.
3. The season is only four weeks long.
4. Data for all four weeks have been entered using standard dBASE III APPEND and EDIT commands.
5. All bowlers bowled every game.

Possible changes in some of these assumptions are explored as exercises in the problems listed at the end of the chapter.

Figures 9.1 through 9.4 show both the structure, and the actual test data, for each relation. (Remember that in dBASE III terminology, each relation is called a database file (.dbf).)

In viewing the data in the BOWLER[1] relation, the observation should be made that the relation holds a large amount of duplication in street addresses and phone numbers. Is the following a valid FD?

phone → stret

```
. list structure
Structure for database : B:sched.dbf
Number of data records :      24
Date of last update    : 05/09/86
Field  Field name  Type      Width    Dec
    1   TNUMB       Numeric       1
    2   WEEK        Numeric       1
    3   LANE        Numeric       1
** Total **                       4
```

(a)

```
. list off
TNUMB WEEK LANE
  1    1    1
  2    1    2
  3    1    4
  4    1    3
  5    1    6
  6    1    5
  1    2    4
  2    2    5
  3    2    2
  4    2    6
  5    2    1
  6    2    3
  1    3    3
  2    3    6
  3    3    1
  4    3    4
  5    3    5
  6    3    2
  1    4    5
  2    4    1
  3    4    3
  4    4    2
  5    4    4
  6    4    6
```

(b)

Figure 9.1   (a) Structure and (b) contents of the SCHED relation.

[1]Relation names will be capitalized, except when using the dBASE III notation relating attributes to the relations they are in, e.g., bowler→bname, which means bname in the BOWLER relation.

```
use team
. list structure
Structure for database : B:team.dbf
Number of data records :        6
Date of last update    : 05/10/86
Field  Field name   Type        Width      Dec
    1  TNUMB        Numeric         1
    2  TNAME        Character      15
    3  CAPTN        Character      15
** Total **                       32
```

(a)

```
list off
TNUMB TNAME              CAPTN
    1 AlleyCats          Ann Jones
    2 Inconsistents      Bill Black
    3 TenPins            Lisa Moore
    4 HiRollers          Jill Miller
    5 Splitters          Roy Lane
    6 SandBaggers        Cindy Fox
    .
    .
```

(b)

Figure 9.2   (a) Structure and (b) contents of the TEAM relation.

If so, the bowler relation is not in BCNF and the original design of the database would be incorrect. It was decided that the proposed FD is not valid for two reasons:

1. There is a distinct possibility that two people with different addresses may have no phone. The word NONE could be used for the phone number in such cases; however, the street address would not be functionally dependent on the phone number.
2. It is possible that the phone number used in the database would be a "phone number at which the bowler can be reached," rather than a "home phone number." This would also cause the FD proposed above to be invalid.

Under these assumptions, some of the stret and phone data present in the BOWLER relation are duplicate, but not redundant.

9.2 ANSWERING SECRETARY QUERIES WITH DBASE III

This section is intended to illustrate the fact that simple queries related to the bowling secretary's database can be answered directly using dBASE III commands, without embedding the commands in the dBASE III program-

```
. use bowler
. list structure
Structure for database : B:bowler.dbf
Number of data records :     24
Date of last update    : 05/20/86
Field  Field name  Type      Width    Dec
    1   BNAME       Character    15
    2   TNUMB       Numeric       1
    3   PHONE       Character     8
    4   STRET       Character    20
    5   STAVG       Numeric       3
** Total **                     48
```
(a)

```
list off
BNAME                TNUMB PHONE     STRET                      STAVG
Jean Adams              5  689-1234  10 Robin St                 111
Steve Adams             5  689-1234  10 Robin St                 130
Bill Black              2  689-2345  15 Bluebird Ln             149
Bonnie Black            2  689-2345  15 Bluebird Ln             120
Bo Blow                 2  NONE      12 Meadowbrook Ln          143
Jo Blow                 2  NONE      12 Meadowbrook Ln           95
Joe Brown               3  689-4567  18 Bluebird Ln             132
Sue Brown               3  689-4567  18 Bluebird Ln             124
Cindy Fox               6  689-5678  19 Cardinal St             103
Randy Fox               6  689-5678  19 Cardinal Ln             147
Ann Jones               1  689-4365  12 Finch Dr                105
John Jones              1  689-4365  12 Finch Dr                143
Joy Lane                5  689-6789  21 Sparrow Ct              125
Roy Lane                5  689-6789  21 Sparrow Ct              167
Jill Miller             4  689-7890  12 Robin St                108
Paul Miller             4  689-7890  12 Robin St                170
Lisa Moore              3  689-8901  11 Lark Dr                 115
Mike Moore              3  689-8901  11 Lark Dr                 140
Jim Smith               1  689-9012  13 Finch Dr                152
Mary Smith              1  689-9012  13 Finch Dr                115
Russel Taylor           6  689-0123  20 Cardinal St             161
Ruth Taylor             6  689-0123  20 Cardinal St             119
Dan White               4  689-2143  16 Robin St                158
Jan White               4  689-2143  16 Robin St                121
```
(b)

Figure 9.3   (a) Structure and (b) contents of the BOWLER relation.

ming language. All query solutions in this section involve the specific relations given in Figures 9.1 through 9.4. In most cases, a sequence of two or more basic commands is required to answer the query. The reader is urged to implement the database, and to execute each set of solutions as they are discussed. If the reader wishes to work in R:base 5000, rather than in dBASE III, he or she should merely read through the queries given in this chapter, and implement the database given in Chapter 10.

The examples given in this section assume that the dBASE III system diskette is in side A on the IBM PC, and that the database relations are in side B. Before executing any of the dBASE III commands, the default disk

```
                    use scores
                  . list structure
                  Structure for database : B:scores.dbf
                  Number of data records :      96
                  Date of last update    : 05/20/86
                  Field   Field name   Type         Width    Dec
                      1   BNAME        Character       15
                      2   WEEK         Numeric          1
                      3   GAME1        Numeric          3
                      4   GAME2        Numeric          3
                      5   GAME3        Numeric          3
                  ** Total **                          26
```
(a)

| . list off for week <= 2 | | | | | . list off for week >= 3 | | | | |
BNAME	WEEK	GAME1	GAME2	GAME3	BNAME	WEEK	GAME1	GAME2	GAME3
Jean Adams	1	119	120	94	Jean Adams	3	123	134	124
Steve Adams	1	112	140	138	Steve Adams	3	134	156	135
Bill Black	1	137	155	155	Bill Black	3	156	165	162
Bonnie Black	1	120	125	115	Bonnie Black	3	123	119	111
Bo Blow	1	160	145	125	Bo Blow	3	165	121	158
Jo Blow	1	101	91	93	Jo Blow	3	89	120	99
Jim Smith	1	160	150	146	Jim Smith	3	164	165	145
Mary Smith	1	120	110	115	Mary Smith	3	112	114	132
Ann Jones	1	98	110	107	Ann Jones	3	108	109	112
John Jones	1	145	150	134	John Jones	3	145	146	144
Joe Brown	1	140	127	129	Joe Brown	3	136	144	125
Sue Brown	1	121	128	124	Sue Brown	3	124	123	119
Cindy Fox	1	119	110	83	Cindy Fox	3	99	110	107
Randy Fox	1	143	150	148	Randy Fox	3	150	161	146
Russel Taylor	1	167	150	166	Russel Taylor	3	189	179	167
Ruth Taylor	1	110	125	122	Ruth Taylor	3	135	112	132
Joy Lane	1	126	127	122	Joy Lane	3	123	132	105
Roy Lane	1	145	180	176	Roy Lane	3	201	202	156
Jill Miller	1	111	101	112	Jill Miller	3	108	112	101
Paul Miller	1	180	196	134	Paul Miller	3	198	167	185
Dan White	1	156	163	154	Dan White	3	161	162	149
Jan White	1	130	125	108	Jan White	3	119	123	141
Lisa Moore	1	99	120	111	Lisa Moore	3	121	107	104
Mike Moore	1	150	149	121	Mike Moore	3	148	148	151
Jean Adams	2	120	125	100	Jean Adams	4	111	121	100
Steve Adams	2	130	146	140	Steve Adams	4	131	127	132
Bill Black	2	154	149	148	Bill Black	4	137	169	154
Bonnie Black	2	120	130	110	Bonnie Black	4	119	121	113
Bo Blow	2	159	135	125	Bo Blow	4	143	157	147
Jo Blow	2	105	91	90	Jo Blow	4	89	99	98
Jim Smith	2	160	160	170	Jim Smith	4	158	163	169
Mary Smith	2	120	110	90	Mary Smith	4	116	117	97
Ann Jones	2	100	110	110	Ann Jones	4	103	68	121
John Jones	2	158	138	135	John Jones	4	148	137	158
Joe Brown	2	139	138	125	Joe Brown	4	130	127	146
Sue Brown	2	126	124	110	Sue Brown	4	124	126	128
Cindy Fox	2	104	90	108	Cindy Fox	4	104	109	110
Randy Fox	2	150	137	163	Randy Fox	4	152	153	154
Russel Taylor	2	160	165	150	Russel Taylor	4	165	158	202
Ruth Taylor	2	130	123	108	Ruth Taylor	4	119	123	117
Joy Lane	2	130	115	120	Joy Lane	4	126	130	128
Roy Lane	2	183	179	138	Roy Lane	4	170	168	186
Jill Miller	2	110	98	103	Jill Miller	4	110	118	105
Paul Miller	2	180	174	178	Paul Miller	4	176	202	181
Dan White	2	161	155	156	Dan White	4	156	149	157
Jan White	2	124	119	130	Jan White	4	124	121	115
Lisa Moore	2	120	102	100	Lisa Moore	4	110	126	106
Mike Moore	2	151	140	125	Mike Moore	4	145	148	162

(b)

Figure 9.4 (a) Structure and (b) contents of the SCORES relation.

should be set to side B within dBASE III. This is done by executing the single command

```
.SET DEFAULT TO B
```

QUERY #1: "What is the name of the captain of team number four?"

This is the simplest of queries, since all of the information required to answer the query is contained in one tuple in one relation. Additionally, only one condition needs to be placed in the query: tnumb $= 4$. The answer to the query is obtained by executing the following commands:

```
.USE team
.LIST OFF captn FOR tnumb = 4
```

The response will be captn $=$ Jill Miller.

QUERY #2: "Find the names of all bowlers with a starting average less than 100."

This query is similar in nature to Query #1 and can be answered with the following sequence:

```
.USE bowler
.LIST OFF bname FOR stavg < 100
```

The response will be bname $=$ Jo Blow.

QUERY #3: "What are the names and phone numbers of all the team members of team number three?"

This query is similar to queries #1 and #2, in that the information to answer the query is located in one relation; however, the solution to this query gives several lines of output, rather than a single value.

```
.USE bowler
.LIST OFF bname,phone FOR tnumb = 3
```

The response will be

bname	phone
Joe Brown	689-4567
Sue Brown	689-4567
Lisa Moore	689-8901
Mike Moore	689-8901

QUERY #4: "On which lane does team number five bowl during the third week of the season?"

This query is only slightly more difficult to answer than those given above. The additional difficulty is caused by the fact that two conditions must be placed on the data being sought. The query is answered with the following sequence of commands:

```
.USE sched
.LIST OFF lane FOR tnumb = 5 .AND. week = 3
```

The response will be lane = 5.

QUERY #5: "Find the names of all bowlers who live on Robin St."

This query requires a search within the stret field of each record in the BOWLER relation to see if the character sequence 'Robin St' appears. This can be accomplished through the use of the $ operator.

```
.USE bowler
.LIST OFF bname FOR 'Robin St' $(stret)
```

The response will yield several names:

> bname
> Jean Adams
> Steve Adams
> Jill Miller
> Paul Miller
> Dan White
> Jan White

When using the $ operator, or any operator or function that pulls a substring out of a longer string of characters, the user must be certain that strings don't exist in the data that would lead to the return of erroneous data. For example, a street address such as '21 BlueRobin St' would give an output value in the last query, even though the street name is 'BlueRobin', not just 'Robin'. One simple way to check this is to return both the name and the street address in the output.

QUERY #6: "How many three-game series greater than 550 have been bowled to date?"

This query can be answered using the COUNT command. The solution also requires a sum to be made within the query.

```
.USE scores
.COUNT FOR game1 + game2 + game3 ) 550
```

The response will be: 2 records. This indicates that only two three-game series greater than 550 have been bowled to date.

QUERY #7: "Who is the captain of the opponents of team number five for week number three?"

The level of skill required to answer this query is considerably higher than that required to answer the previous queries; data obtained from one relation must be used in a second relation, in order to obtain the desired result. To answer this query, the bowling secretary must first use the answer to Query #4 to determine the lane to which team number five is assigned on week three. The answer here is lane = 5. Since opponents are assigned to adjacent lanes, the secretary must deduce that the opponents of team five will be on lane six. Using this last piece of information, the tnumb of the opponents of team number five on week number three can be answered with the following sequence:

```
.LIST OFF tnumb FOR lane = 6 .AND. week = 3
```

The response will be tnumb = 2. The name of the opponent's captain can now be determined by

```
.USE team
.LIST OFF captn FOR tnumb = 2
```

The overall query answer will be returned as captn = Bill Black.

Query #7 can be answered in a variety of ways. The solution outlined above is probably the most straightforward and easiest to understand for a beginning user of dBASE III. A second solution involves the use of the JOIN relational operator. (See Appendix A if a review of the JOIN operator is required.)

The first portion of the second solution to Query #7 is the same as that given above: The lane assignment for team five during week three must be found (as lane = 5). From this it must again be deduced that the opponent's lane is six. Next, the following sequence of commands must be executed:

```
.CLEAR ALL
.SELECT 2
.USE team
.SELECT 1
```

```
.USE sched
.JOIN WITH team TO result;
   FOR lane = 6 .AND. week = 3 .AND.;
      tnumb = team − )tnumb;
   FIELDS team − )captn
.USE result
.LIST OFF
.USE
.ERASE result
```

The basic difference between the two solutions to Query #7 is that the JOIN was done explicitly in the second version, while in the first version the JOIN was done mentally by the secretary.

In the last solution, the CLEAR ALL command was used to avoid an ALIAS error, which might occur in setting up work areas 1 and 2 with the associated SELECT commands. (This error would occur if either TEAM or SCHED had been USE'd in earlier queries.) The single USE command in the next-to-last statement closes the result.dbf file, that was just created, so that it can be ERASE'd without error by the next command. A .dbf file cannot be ERASE'd when it is open.

QUERY #8: "How many total pins (without handicap) does Bill Black have at the end of week number three?"

All the information required to answer this query can be found in the SCORES relation; however, the solution looks complicated because an arithmetic calculation must be made both within, and across, tuples. The solution is made relatively simple through the use of the SUM function:

```
.USE scores
.SUM game1 + game2 + game3 TO total;
   FOR bname = 'Bill Black' .AND. week ⟨ = 3
.? total
```

The result is returned as total = 1381.

QUERY #9: "List the names of all league members who are not team members of the SandBaggers."

This query is most easily answered with the JOIN command. (Users must always be careful, when using the JOIN, that large numbers of tuples are not generated in the process. In the worst case, if a relation with "m" tuples is JOINed with a relation with "n" tuples, m times n tuples could be generated.) The desired result fo Query #9 can be generated by

```
.CLEAR ALL
.SELECT 2
.USE team
.SELECT 1
.USE bowler
.JOIN WITH team TO result FOR team −⟩tname  =  'SandBaggers';
   .AND. tnumb ⟨⟩ team −⟩tnumb FIELDS bowler −⟩bname
.USE result
.LIST OFF
.USE
.ERASE result
```

The output here will be twenty names.

QUERY #10: "During week number three, which bowlers bowled a better three-game series than Lisa Moore (without handicaps)?"

This query can be answered in a two-step process: step one is to determine the three-game series score for Lisa Moore on week three; step two is to find the names of those people who exceeded this score on week three. One solution is

```
.CLEAR ALL
.USE scores
LIST OFF game1 + game2 + game3 FOR bname  =  'Lisa Moore';
   .AND. week  =  3
```

The result here is a three-game score of 332.

```
.LIST OFF bname FOR game1 + game2 + game3 ⟩ 332 ;
   .AND. week  =  3
```

The final answer is a list of nineteen names.

9.3 THE MAIN MENU FOR PREPROGRAMMED
QUERY SOLUTIONS

The previous section detailed the solutions to some fairly simple queries. It is assumed that the bowling secretary would enter the commands for these type of solutions directly from the terminal. As the queries become more complicated, the sequence of commands required for the solution of the queries is too long and involved to be entered directly by the secretary. In these cases, the list of potentially useful queries can be placed in a menu, and the menu displayed to the secretary on the computer terminal. When the secretary chooses one of the queries, a program written in dBASE III's programming language is executed to answer the query. The following sections in this chapter examine such a menu in detail. The particular queries placed in the menu are ones that are deemed reasonable, but the list of queries is not exhaustive, and can be expanded with relative ease.

The sample menu, as seen by the secretary when the program executes, is given in Figure 9.5. The mainline program module that displays this menu, and accepts the query choice, is named "sdbmain.prg." This module is displayed in Figure 9.6. Each of the first five menu choices results in the execution of a different program module. Some of these second layer modules call other modules to perform minor tasks. All program modules that are involved in using the main menu are discussed in detail in the following sections in this chapter.

The logic contained in sdbmain.prg repeats the following sequence until the choice picked is a "6," which terminates execution.

1. Display the main menu.
2. Wait for an input choice.
3. If the choice entered was valid then
    Transfer control to the appropriate program module
Else
    Print out an error message; delay for about two
    seconds; and return to 2 above.

```
MONDAY NIGHT IRREGULARS BOWLING LEAGUE QUERY MENU
=================================================

    1 - DISPLAY STATISTICS FOR AN INDIVIDUAL BOWLER

    2 - DISPLAY TOTAL PINS FOR EACH TEAM

    3 - DISPLAY TEAM STANDINGS

    4 - DISPLAY SCHEDULE FOR A GIVEN WEEK

    5 - GENERATE AN END-OF-SEASON REPORT

    6 - RETURN TO DBASE III COMMAND LEVEL


Enter your choice
```

Figure 9.5   Main menu of the bowling secretary's database.

```
. type dsdbmain.prg
******************MAINLINE PROGRAM FOR SECRETARY'S DATABASE**************
* Program name is: " sdbmain.prg"
* Written by Glenn A. Jackson
* Oakland University, Rochester, MI 48063
* Bowling leagues may use this program -- at their own risk!!!
*
CLEAR
SET TALK OFF
CLOSE DATABASES
SET DEFAULT TO B
PUBLIC max_wk,bavg,hndkp,saveit
*
*
* List the query menu for the user and accept the next query choice
*
*
DO WHILE .t.
   CLEAR
   @  5,10 SAY 'MONDAY NIGHT IRREGULARS BOWLING LEAGUE QUERY MENU'
   @  6,10 SAY '==================================================='
   @  9,10 SAY ' 1 - DISPLAY STATISTICS FOR AN INDIVIDUAL BOWLER'
   @ 11,10 SAY ' 2 - DISPLAY TOTAL PINS FOR EACH TEAM'
   @ 13,10 SAY ' 3 - DISPLAY TEAM STANDINGS'
   @ 15,10 SAY ' 4 - DISPLAY SCHEDULE FOR A GIVEN WEEK'
   @ 17,10 SAY ' 5 - GENERATE AN END-OF-SEASON REPORT'
   @ 19,10 SAY ' 6 - RETURN TO DBASE III COMMAND LEVEL'
   @ 22,10 SAY ' Enter your choice'
   WAIT ' ' TO choice
   DO CASE
      CASE choice = '1'
         STORE 'SDB' TO eos_check
         DO b:bwlrst
      CASE choice = '2'
         DO b:teampns
      CASE choice = '3'
         DO b:teamstd
      CASE choice = '4'
         DO b:wkschdl
      CASE choice = '5'
         DO b:eosrpt
      CASE choice = '6'
         CLEAR
         CLOSE DATABASES
         @ 5,10 SAY "THE SECRETARY'S DATABASE HAS BEEN CLOSED"
         @ 6,10 SAY 'YOU ARE BEING RETURNED TO DBASEIII COMMAND LEVEL'
         SET DEFAULT TO A
         SET TALK ON
         RETURN
      OTHERWISE
         @ 22,10 SAY 'YOU HAVE ENTERED AN INVALID ENTRY!!!!'
         DO b:delay
   ENDCASE
   CLOSE DATABASES
ENDDO
```

Figure 9.6   The main program module for the secretary's database: sdbmain.prg.

Delay.prg is a short program module that is called by sdbmain.prg when a two-second delay is required. A copy of delay.prg is given in Figure 9.7. This program does nothing but increment a counter around loop enough times to consume about two seconds of time.

```
      type delay.prg
      *************** TWO SECOND DELAY MODULE ***************
      *
      *Program module name is "delay.prg"
      *Written by Glenn A. Jackson
      *Oakland University, Rochester, MI 48063
      *
      *
      *This module gives an approximate two second delay before
      * returning to the calling program
      *
      *This module is called by: sdbmain.prg
      *
      STORE 0 TO delay_ctr
      DO WHILE delay_ctr < 50
         STORE delay_ctr + 1 TO delay_ctr
      ENDDO
      RETURN
```

Figure 9.7   The two-second delay module: delay.prg.

9.4 PROGRAM MODULE BWLRST.PRG

This module is called by sdbmain.prg when the main menu choice is "1—DISPLAY STATISTICS FOR AN INDIVIDUAL BOWLER." The execution of this module results in the calculation and output of the statistics for a given bowler at the end of a given week in the season. The module asks for the desired week for which the statistics are desired and the bowler's name. The module checks to make certain that both the name and the week are valid values. The general logic of the module is outlined in Figure 9.8 and the dBASE III implementation is given in Figure 9.9. A typical output from the module is found in Figure 9.10 (p. 121).

Two points related to bwlrst.prg may need further clarification. The first deals with the two "IF eos_check = 'SDB' " statements that appear in the module. Bwlrst.prg is called from two different program modules: sdbmain.prg and eosrpt.prg. When bwlrst:prg is called from sdbmain.prg, the entire module is executed. When bwlrst.prg is called from eosrpt.prg, much of the module's logic is skipped, since the name of the bowler and the desired week are already known in this latter case. Before bwlrst.prg is called from sdbmain.prg, the value in eos_check is set to 'SDB,' while eos_check is set to 'EOS' before bwlrst.prg is called from eosrpt.prg.

The second point of clarification deals with the calculation of handicaps. The handicap is defined as being three-fourths of the difference between a bowler's current average and 200, with no negative handicaps allowed. The bowler's current average and the bowler's handicap are integers

```
LOGIC IF eos_check = 'SDB' WHEN BWLRST.PRG IS EXECUTED:


    1.  Execute findwk.prg to find the last week for which
        game scores have been entered into the SCORES
        relation.  The value is returned as "max_wk."

    2.  Input the week of the season for which statistics
        are desired  as "wk," and check the value for
        validity.

    3.  Input the name of the bowler whose statistics are
        desired as "name," and check the value for
        validity.

    4.  For each tuple in the SCORES relation in which the
        bname attribute value equals name, and the week
        attribute value is less than or equal to wk:

            a)  Check game1, game2, and game3 to see
                if any have higher values than the current
                hi_game score;  if so, save that value as
                hi_game;

            b)  Check the sum of game1, game2, and game3
                to see if the sum is higher than the current
                hi_series value;  if so, save the sum as
                hi_series;

            c)  Add the sum of game1, game2, and game3
                to tot_pins.

    5.  Calculate this bowler's average and handicap and
        save them as "bavg" and "hndkp," respectively.

    6.  Ouput the results.



LOGIC IF eos_check = 'EOS' WHEN BWLRST.PRG IS EXECUTED:


    Sections 1, 2, 3, and  6 above are skipped.  Only
    sections 4 and 5 are executed.
```

Figure 9.8   General logic for program module bwlrst.prg.

that are obtained by truncation, not rounding. If truncation were not used in both cases the league standings would be greatly affected.

9.5 PROGRAM MODULE TEAMPNS.PRG

This module is called by sdbmain.prg when the main menu choice is "2—DISPLAY TOTAL PINS FOR EACH TEAM." This program module calls findwk.prg to determine the last week for which data have been entered into the SCORES relation, and then proceeds to determine and print out

```
. type bwlrst.prg
*********************************************************************
*Procedure name is: "bwlrst.prg"
*Written by Glenn A. Jackson
*Oakland University, Rochester, MI 48063
*
*This procedure calculates and outputs the following statistics
*on an individual bowler: High-series, High-game, Total pins,
*average and handicap.  All statistics include all games bowled
*to date.
*
*Procedure is called by sdbmain.prg
*
CLEAR
*
*Initialize running sum variables and counting variables
*
STORE 0 TO hi_series,tot_pins,hi_game
STORE 1 TO ctr
SELECT 1
USE b:scores
*
* Run this next section of code only if called from the main
*   menu.
*
IF eos_check = 'SDB'
*
*Find last week for which scores have been entered -- as max_wk
*
DO b:findwk
*
  STORE '   ' TO wk
  DO WHILE .t.
     @ 7,15 SAY 'IF YOU WISH THE STATISTICS FOR THE SEASON TO DATE'
     @ 8,15 SAY 'ENTER '+STR(max_wk,2)+ ;
                ', THE LAST WEEK FOR WHICH DATA WERE ENTERED'
     @ 9,15 SAY 'OTHERWISE, ENTER THE WEEK DESIRED.'
     @ 11,15 GET wk
     READ
     IF VAL(wk) > max_wk .OR. VAL(wk) < 1
        @ 15,10 SAY 'THE WEEK INPUT IS INVALID!!!!'
        DO b:delay
        STORE '   ' TO wk
        CLEAR
     ELSE
        CLEAR
        EXIT
     ENDIF
*
  ENDDO
*Enter the bowler's name and make certain it is valid
*
  STORE '                 ' TO name
*
```

Figure 9.9   (a) First half of program module bwlrst.prg.

the total number of "scratch" pins for each team. A sample output from
teampns.prg is given in Figure 9.11. The general logic for teampns.prg is
given in Figure 9.12 and the module itself is shown in Figure 9.13 (p. 122).

When making any JOIN in a database program, care must be taken

```
    DO WHILE .t.
       @ 7,20 SAY "ENTER THE BOWLER'S NAME, e.g. Joe Jones"
       @ 8,20 GET name
       READ
       COUNT FOR bname = name TO check
       IF check = 0
          @ 12,20 SAY 'THE NAME ENTERED IS NOT IN THE DATABASE'
          @ 13,20 SAY 'CHECK IT AND RE-ENTER'
          DO b:delay
          STORE '                    ' TO name
          CLEAR
       ELSE
          EXIT
       ENDIF
    ENDDO
ENDIF
*
GOTO TOP
DO WHILE ctr <= VAL(wk)
   LOCATE FOR bname = name .AND. week = ctr
   IF game1 > hi_game
      STORE game1 TO hi_game
   ENDIF
   IF game2 > hi_game
      STORE game2 TO hi_game
   ENDIF
   IF game3 > hi_game
      STORE game3 TO hi_game
   ENDIF
   STORE game1 + game2 + game3 TO tot3
   STORE tot_pins + tot3 TO tot_pins
   IF tot3 > hi_series
      STORE tot3 TO hi_series
   ENDIF
   STORE ctr + 1 TO ctr
ENDDO
*
STORE INT(tot_pins/(VAL(wk)*3)) TO bavg
IF bavg < 200
   STORE INT((200 - bavg)* 0.75) TO hndkp
ELSE
   STORE 0 TO hndkp
ENDIF
*
*Do this section only if called from main menu
*
IF eos_check = 'SDB'
   CLEAR
   @ 7,20 SAY 'STATISTICS FOR '+ TRIM(bname) + ' THRU WEEK ' + wk
   @ 8,20 SAY '=====================================' 
   @ 10,20 SAY 'AVERAGE PINS PER GAME: '+ STR(bavg,3)
   @ 12,20 SAY 'TOTAL PINS - WITHOUT HANDICAP: ' + STR(tot_pins,4)
   @ 14,20 SAY 'HIGH GAME SCORE TO DATE: ' + STR(hi_game,3)
   @ 16,20 SAY 'HIGH SERIES TO DATE: ' + STR(hi_series,3)
   @ 18,20 SAY 'CURRENT HANDICAP: ' + STR(hndkp,3)
   @ 22,20 SAY '  '
   WAIT
   CLEAR
ENDIF
RETURN
```

Figure 9.9   (b) Second half of program module bwlrst.prg.

```
                              STATISTICS FOR Jean Adams THRU WEEK 3
                              =========================================

                              AVERAGE PINS PER GAME: 117

                              TOTAL PINS - WITHOUT HANDICAP: 1059

                              HIGH GAME SCORE TO DATE: 134

                              HIGH SERIES TO DATE: 381
```

Figure 9.10 Typical output from the execution of main menu choice "1."

```
                              CURRENT HANDICAP:  62
```

```
         TOTAL  SCRATCH  PINS  THROUGH  WEEK   4
         =========================================
         TEAM NO.    TEAM NAME          TOTAL PINS
         --------    ---------          ----------

            1        AlleyCats             6257
            2        Inconsistents         6172
            3        TenPins               6147
            4        HiRollers             6798
            5        Splitters             6580
            6        SandBaggers           6534
```

Figure 9.11 Sample output from the execution of program module teampns.prg.

```
1.  Execute findwk.prg to determine the last week for
    which scores have been entered into the SCORES
    relation.

2.  Output the header for the data that will be output
    below.

3.  For each team (using the variable "ctr" as both
    team number and loop counter), DO the following:

    a)  JOIN the SCORES and BOWLER relations, where
        bowler->tnumb = the selected team number and
        bowler->bname = scores->bname to form a new
        relation, TEMP2, keeping only the game1,
        game2, and game3 attributes (FIELDs).
        TEMP2 will hold all the game scores for one
        team  through the current week in the season.

    b)  Use the TEAM relation to determine the name of the
        team being evaluated using the team number as the
        identifying value.  Save the team name as "name."

    c)  Use the TEMP2 relation to sum the game scores
        for this team, and output the total team pins.

    d)  ERASE the temporary relation temp2.dbf from
        the database.

    e)  Increment the team number (ctr) to the next
        value.
```

Figure 9.12 General logic for program module teampns.prg.

```
type teampns.prg
*************************************************************
*Procedure name is "teampns.prg"
*Written by Glenn A. Jackson
*Oakland University, Rochester, MI 48063
*
*This procedure prints out the total number of "scratch" pins
*for each team for the season to date.
*
*Procedure is called by sdbmain.prg
*
CLEAR
CLOSE DATABASES
SELECT 1
USE b:bowler
SELECT 2
USE b:scores
*Find last week for which scores have been entered - return as max_wk.
DO b:findwk
*
*Print out the header for the output data.
*
@ 5,20 SAY 'TOTAL  SCRATCH  PINS  THROUGH  WEEK ' + STR(max_wk,3)
@ 6,20 SAY '====================================='
@ 7,20 SAY 'TEAM NO.    TEAM NAME          TOTAL PINS'
@ 8,20 SAY '--------    ----------         ----------'
*
*Calculate and print out the data
*
STORE 1 TO ctr
DO WHILE ctr <= 6
   SELECT bowler
   JOIN WITH scores TO b:temp2 FOR tnumb = ctr .AND. ;
       bname = scores->bname FIELDS game1,game2,game3
   SELECT 3
   USE b:team
   LOCATE FOR tnumb = ctr
   STORE tname TO name
   SELECT 4
   USE b:temp2
   SUM game1,game2,game3 TO gm1,gm2,gm3
   @ 9+ctr,20 SAY STR(ctr,4) + '        '+ name + '        ' + STR(gm1+gm2+gm3)
   USE
ERASE b:temp2.dbf
   STORE ctr+1 to ctr
ENDDO
@ 22,10 SAY ' '
WAIT
RETURN
```

Figure 9.13   The program module teampns.prg.

to assure that the result of the JOIN will not be a relation that is too large to store in the space available on the disk being used. In the JOIN used in teampns.prg, the relation generated, TEMP2, will always have

(3 games/week) * (4 bowlers/team) * (N weeks bowled)

tuples. If it were the fourth week in the season, $N = 4$, each construction of TEMP2 would result in the generation of 48 tuples.

```
  type findwk.prg
*********************** FINDWK.PRG ***************************
*
*Module name is "findwk.prg"
*Written by Glenn A. Jackson
*Oakland University, Rochester, MI 48063
*
*This module determines the largest week value that has been
*entered in the week attribute field in either the
*scores.dbf or sched.dbf relation.  The module assumes that
*either scores.dbf or sched.dbf is the active database when
*the module is executed.
*
*Called by the following modules:
* bwlrst.prg, teampns.prg, teamstd.prg, wkschdl.prg and eosrpt.prg
*
*The highest week value is returned as the integer variable: max_wk
*
@ 10,15 SAY "MAKING SOME CALCULATIONS -- DON'T GO AWAY !"
max_wk = 0
GOTO TOP
DO WHILE .NOT. EOF()
  IF week > max_wk
    max_wk = week
  ENDIF
  SKIP
ENDDO
*
CLEAR
RETURN
```

Figure 9.14   The program module findwk.prg.

Teampns.prg calls findwk.prg to determine the last week in the season for which scores have been entered into the SCORES relation. This module is given in Figure 9.14. The logic in this module needs one point of clarification. The purpose of the module is to locate the largest week attribute value from the current active database file. This means that the relation (.dbf) to be searched must be activated prior to the execution of findwk.prg. Since both the SCORES and SCHED relations have week as an attribute field, either one of these relations can be made active prior to the calling of findwk.prg. If SCORES is the active relation, the week value determined is "the last week for which game scores have been entered into the database"; however, if SCHED is the active relation, the week value determined is "the last week in the bowling season." Findwk.prg is used to determine both of these week values.

9.6 PROGRAM MODULE WKSCHDL.PRG

This program module is called by sdbmain.prg when the main menu choice is "4—DISPLAY SCHEDULE FOR A GIVEN WEEK." The execution of this module results in the output of a table giving the team names, and the lanes to which each team has been assigned, for a given week in the bowling season. The module requests the desired week of the season as an input, stores this value as "inval," and verifies that the input value is valid, before proceeding.

A typical output from the execution of this module is given in Figure 9.15. The logic contained in the module is given in Figure 9.16, and the module itself is displayed in Figure 9.17.

The heart of the implementation is again a JOIN that creates a temporary relation, TEMP1. In this case, the TEAM and SCHED relations are joined over the tnumb attribute, so that the team name can be used in the output, rather than the team number.

```
THE SCHEDULE FOR WEEK NUMBER 2
===============================
TEAM                 LANE NUMBER
----                 -----------
AlleyCats                4
Inconsistents            5
TenPins                  2
HiRollers                6
Splitters                1
SandBaggers              3
```

Figure 9.15 Typical output from program module wkschdl.prg.

```
1.  Execute findwk.prg to find the last week in the
    season.  The last week value is returned as "max_wk."
    (Note that the SCHED relation is placed into USE
    prior to the calling of findwk.prg, so that SCHED
    is the relation seached by findwk.prg.)

2.  Input a value for the week for which the schedule is
    desired, as "inval," and verify that the week
    requested is a valid one.  Repeat this process
    until the week is valid.

3.  JOIN the TEAM and SCHED relations where sched->week =
    inval, and sched->tnumb = team->tnumb, to form a
    new relation, TEMP1, keeping only the tname and
    lane attributes.

4.  Output the data header.

5.  Output the tname and lane values from TEMP1.

6.  ERASE the TEMP1 relation from the database.
```

Figure 9.16 General logic for program module wkschdl.prg.

FIGURE 9.17 The program module wkschdl.prg.

```
. type wkschdl.prg
****************************************************************
*
*Procedure name is "wkschdl.prg"
*Written by Glenn A. Jackson
*Oakland University, Rochester, MI 48063
*
*This procedure prints out the schedule for a given week.
*
*Input is the week of the season for which the schedule is *desired.
*Output is the schedule giving team name and lane assignment.
*
*Procedure is called by sdbmain.prg
*
*
CLEAR
CLOSE DATABASES
SELECT 1
USE b:sched
STORE '    ' TO inval
*
*Find last week in the season -- value returned as max_wk
*
DO b:findwk
*
DO WHILE .t.
   @ 7,10 SAY 'ENTER WEEK FOR WHICH SCHEDULE IS DESIRED'
   @ 9,10 SAY 'ONLY VALUES BETWEEN 1 AND '+ STR(max_wk,2) + ' ALLOWED'
   @ 11,10 GET inval
   READ
   IF VAL(inval) > max_wk .OR. VAL(inval) < 1
      @ 15,10 SAY 'THE WEEK INPUT IS INVALID !!!!!'
      DO b:delay
      STORE '    ' TO inval
      CLEAR
   ELSE
      EXIT
   ENDIF
ENDDO
*
@ 15,10 SAY 'PLEASE WAIT----CALCULATIONS BEING MADE!!!'
SELECT 2
USE team
SELECT sched
JOIN WITH team TO b:temp1 FOR week = VAL(inval) .AND. ;
         tnumb = team->tnumb FIELDS team->tname, lane
*
*Output the schedule to the screen
*
CLEAR
@ 5,10 SAY '          THE SCHEDULE FOR WEEK NUMBER '+ inval
@ 6,10 SAY '          ================================'
@ 7,10 SAY '          TEAM                LANE NUMBER'
@ 8,10 SAY '          ----                -----------'
*
SELECT 3
USE b:temp1
GOTO TOP
STORE 9 TO lineno
DO WHILE .NOT. EOF()
   @ lineno,10 SAY '        ' + tname + '           '+ STR(lane,2)
   STORE lineno+1 TO lineno
   SKIP
ENDDO
@ 22,10 SAY '  '
WAIT
CLEAR
CLOSE DATABASES
ERASE b:temp1.dbf
RETURN
```

125

9.7 PROGRAM MODULE EOSRPT.PRG

This program module is called by sdbmain.prg when the main menu choice is "5—GENERATE AN END-OF-SEASON REPORT." The execution of this module results in the determination and output of the names of the bowlers who (1) had the highest single game score for the season, (2) had the highest three-game series for the season, and (3) ended the season with the highest average.

The output from this module for the data in the database is given in Figure 9.18. The logic contained in the module is given in Figure 9.19, and the module itself is displayed in Figure 9.20.

A somewhat out-of-the-ordinary feature of eosrpt.prg is the way in which the names of the bowlers who have the same highest score in a given category are saved. The names of the bowlers with the highest score in a given category are stored in a unary relation related to that category. The names of these specially created relations are HIGHGAM, HIGHSER, and HIGHAVG. The relations are unary because each relation has only one attribute, bname. As each bowler's scores are analyzed, if their score is found to be equal to the one that is currently felt to be the highest, that bowler's name is APPENDED to the appropriate relation. If the bowler's score is found to be higher than the value that was thought to be the highest, the relation is ZAPed to eliminate old values and the new name is then APPENDed. These three relations must be created before the program is executed, but each relation is always unpopulated when the execution of eosrpt.prg begins. All tuples are ERASEd from the three relations before eosrpt.prg terminates. Just before they are ERASEd, the contents of each of the three relations are output using a short program module named file-

```
        END-OF-SEASON REPORT
        =====================

HIGHEST SINGLE GAME SCORE OF 202
WAS BOWLED BY THE FOLLOWING BOWLER(S):
        Roy Lane
        Paul Miller
        Russel Taylor

HIGHEST THREE GAME SERIES OF 559
WAS BOWLED BY THE FOLLOWING BOWLER(S):
        Roy Lane
        Paul Miller

HIGHEST SEASON PER GAME AVERAGE OF 179
WAS BOWLED BY THE FOLLOWING BOWLER(S):
        Paul Miller
```

Figure 9.18   Output of eosrpt.prg for the data in the sample database.

1. Execute program module findwk.prg to determine the last week in the bowling season. The last week value is returned as "max_wk."

2. Initialize pertinent variables.

3. DO the following logic as long as there are tuples left in the BOWLER relation.

   a) Save the bname value from the current bowler tuple in "name."

   b) Execute program module bwlrst.prg (after setting variable eos_check to 'EOS') to determine the highest single game score, highest three-game series score, and the end-of-season average for this one bowler. These values are returned in variables "hi_game," "hi_series," and "bavg," respectively.

   c) The highest single game score for all bowlers is stored in "best_game"; thus, if hi_game > best_game, save hi_game as best_game, and save the bowler's name in HIGHGAM after eliminating previous names. If hi_game = best_game, save the bowler's name in HIGHGAM.

   The highest three game series score for all bowlers is stored in "best_series"; thus if hi_series > best_series, save hi_series as best_series, and save the bowler's name in HIGHSER after eliminating previous names. If hi_series = best_series, save the bowler's name in HIGHSER.

   The highest average for all bowlers is stored in "best_avg"; thus if bavg > best_avg, save bavg as best_avg, and save the bowler's name in HIGHAVG after eliminating previous names. If bavg > best_avg, save the bowler's name in HIGHAVG.

4. Output the final values.

Figure 9.19   General logic of program module eosrpt.prg.

out.prg. A listing of fileout.prg and the exact structure for each of the special relations are given at the end of the chapter.

9.8 PROGRAM MODULE TEAMSTD.PRG

This module is called by sdbmain.prg when the main menu choice is "3—DISPLAY TEAM STANDINGS." The execution of this module results in the output of the won–lost record of each team for a given week in the bowling season. The module begins by requesting the week of the season for which the standings are desired. After making certain that the week

```
type eosrpt.prg
*****************************************************************
*Procedure name is "eosrpt.prg".
*Written by Glenn A. Jackson
*Oakland University, Rochester, MI 48063
*
*This procedure calculates and prints out the end-of-season
* report.
*Procedure is called by sdbmain.prg.
*This procedure calls bwlrst.prg
*
CLEAR
*Some data will be returned from "bwlrst.prg" using PUBLIC
* variables.
PUBLIC name, hi_series, hi_game, bavg, eos_check, fname, wk
*
@ 5,10 SAY 'BE PATIENT -- THIS WILL TAKE SOME TIME !!!!!'
*
SELECT 2
USE b:sched
*
*Find last week in the season -- value returned as max_wk.
*
DO b:findwk
*
SELECT 3
USE b:bowler
GOTO TOP
STORE 0 TO best_series, best_game, best_avg
SET SAFETY OFF
DO WHILE .NOT. EOF()
  STORE bname TO name
  STORE STR(max_wk,2) TO wk
  STORE 'EOS' TO eos_check
  DO b:bwlrst
  SELECT 4
*
  IF hi_game > best_game
    STORE hi_game TO best_game
    USE b:highgam
    ZAP
    APPEND BLANK
    REPLACE bname WITH name
    USE
  ELSE
    IF hi_game = best_game
    USE b:highgam
    APPEND BLANK
    REPLACE bname WITH name
    USE
    ENDIF
  ENDIF
*
  IF hi_series > best_series
    STORE hi_series TO best_series
    USE b:highser
    ZAP
    APPEND BLANK
    REPLACE bname WITH name
    USE
  ELSE
```

Figure 9.20 (a) First half of program module eosrpt.prg.

```
     IF hi_series = best_series
     USE b:highser
     APPEND BLANK
     REPLACE bname WITH name
     USE
     ENDIF
   ENDIF
*
   IF bavg > best_avg
     STORE bavg TO best_avg
     USE b:highavg
     ZAP
     APPEND BLANK
     REPLACE bname WITH name
     USE
   ELSE
     IF bavg = best_avg
     USE b:highavg
     APPEND BLANK
     REPLACE bname WITH name
     USE
     ENDIF
   ENDIF
*
   SELECT bowler
   SKIP
ENDDO
*Print out header for end-of-season output
*
@ 5,25 SAY 'END-OF-SEASON REPORT'
@ 6,25 SAY '===================='
@ 8,20 SAY 'HIGHEST SINGLE GAME SCORE OF ' + STR(best_game,3)
@ 9,20 SAY 'WAS BOWLED BY THE FOLLOWING BOWLER(S): '
STORE "b:highgam" TO fname
DO b:fileout
*
@ ROW()+2,20 SAY 'HIGHEST THREE GAME SERIES OF ' + STR(best_series,3)
@ ROW()+1,20 SAY 'WAS BOWLED BY THE FOLLOWING BOWLER(S): '
STORE "b:highser" TO fname
DO b:fileout
*
@ ROW()+2,20 SAY 'HIGHEST SEASON PER GAME AVERAGE OF ' + STR(best_avg,3)
@ ROW()+1,20 SAY 'WAS BOWLED BY THE FOLLOWING BOWLER(S): '
STORE "b:highavg" TO fname
DO b:fileout
*
@ 24,20 SAY '  '
WAIT
SET SAFETY ON
RETURN


B>
```

Figure 9.20   (b) Second half of program module eosrpt.prg.

entered is valid, the program calculates the won–lost record for each team and prints out the standings in tabular form. The total pins for each team are also output.

Figure 9.21 shows the team standings at the end of week two for the data stored in the sample database. Figure 9.22 gives the general logic of the module, while Figure 9.23 shows the actual module. This program module is by far the most complex module in the implementation, and requires a great deal of time to execute. The approximate time required to calculate the standings for week one is four minutes, while the time required to calculate the standings for week four is twelve minutes! The reason for the drastic increase in time between the first and the fourth week is that the summary data are not stored from one week to the next. Thus, in order to calculate the standings for week four, the standings for weeks one, two, and three must be recalculated. This fact is a direct result of the design decision, made in Chapter 5, to not store data in the database that could be calculated from other attributes in the database. In light of the large time values involved, this design decision should undoubtedly be reevaluated. (It would take about one hour to calculate the standings for the fifteenth week in the season!) Some suggestions for shortening the execution time are contained in the problems at the end of this chapter.

Teamstd.prg makes use of another permanent "extra" relation, T_STATS, that was not a part of the original database design. This relation has four attributes: tnumb, wins, losses, and totpins. When this relation is created, the tnumb values are set to 1 through 6, the numbers of the teams in the league, and all other attribute values are set to zero. All attribute values, except the tnumb's, are set back to zero before the execution of teamstd.prg is terminated.

T_STATS always has only six tuples, one for each team in the league, with tnumb as the primary key. As the execution of teamstd.prg progress, making calculations on a week-by-week and team-by-team basis, the values in T_STATS are adjusted accordingly.

```
            MONDAY NIGHT IRREGULARS BOWLING LEAGUE
            TEAM STANDINGS AT THE END OF WEEK NUMBER 2
            ===========================================

      TEAM NAME         WINS         LOSSES          TOTAL PINS
      ---------         ----         ------          ----------
      AlleyCats         5.0          3.0             3106
      Inconsistents     2.0          6.0             3038
      TenPins           1.0          7.0             3019
      HiRollers         7.0          1.0             3358
      Splitters         6.5          1.5             3225
      SandBaggers       2.5          5.5             3181
```

Figure 9.21 Team standings at the end of week two, as output by teamstd.prg.

1. Execute findwk.prg to determine the last week for which scores have been entered into the SCORES relation. The last week value is returned as "max_wk."

2. Input the value of the week for which standings are desired, as "in_wk," and verify that the week requested is valid. Repeat this process until a valid value of in_wk has been entered.

3. For each lane (noted as ln), DO the following for each week (noted as wk):

    a) JOIN the SCHED and BOWLER relations where sched->week = wk, sched->lane = ln and sched->tnumb = bowler->tnumb, to form a new relation, NAMES, keeping only the bname, tnumb, and stavg attributes. (NAMES will hold the names of all bowlers from the team that bowled on a given lane on a given week in the season.)

    b) For each bowler, whose name appears in NAMES, DO the following:

        Locate the tuple in SCORES for this bowler and this week;

        Determine this bowler's handicap for this week;

        Add this bowler's individual game scores to the team totals for each game (including the current handicap). The code used here is: G1A is the total pins for game1 for the team on an odd-numbered lane, while G1B is the total pins for game1 for the team on the opponent's even-numbered lane. G2A, G3A, G2B, and G3B have similar meaning.

        REPLACE totpins in T_STATS with the old value of totpins plus the sum of this bowler's three game scores (without handicap).

        Adjust the won and lost records for the last two teams analyzed. The coding here is that the team on the odd-numbered lane has its identifiers ending with "A," or "a," while the team on the even-numbered lane has identifiers that end in "B," or "b."

4. JOIN the T_STATS and TEAM relations where t_stats->tnumb = team->tnumb to form a new relation, STATS, keeping only the wins, losses, tname, and totpins attributes.

5. Output the league standings from STATS.

6. ERASE STATS and zero-out the appropriate attributes in T_STATS.

Figure 9.22   General logic for program module teamstd.prg.

9.9 STRUCTURE OF THE TEMPORARY RELATIONS

Program modules eosrpt.prg and teamstd.prg use several relations that are not part of the designed database. These relations are referred to as being **temporary relations**, since their contents are meaningful only during the execution of a given program module. Their contents are continually being created and destroyed, and their contents are not valid once the program module that uses them terminates execution.

```
B>type teamstd.prg
************************************************************
*Procedure name is "teamstd.prg"
*Written by Barbara A. MacNeil
*Modified by Glenn A. Jackson
*Oakland University, Rochester, MI 48063
*
*This procedure calculates and prints out the league standings
* for any week.  The week is input from the terminal.
*
*Procedure is called by sdbmain.prg
*
*This procedure uses several temporary relations to store
* intermediate data required in the calculations.  These
* relations are discussed in Section 9.##.
*
*This procedure calls b:hndkp_avg.prg
*
CLEAR
SELECT 1
USE b:scores
SELECT 2
USE b:bowler
SELECT 3
USE b:t_stats INDEX b:numb
SELECT 4
USE b:sched
SELECT 5
USE b:team
*
*Find last week for which scores have been entered -- as max_wk
*
SELECT scores
DO b:findwk
*
*Enter the week for which the standings are desired -- as in_wk.
*
STORE '  ' TO in_wk
DO WHILE .t.
   @ 7,15 SAY 'IF YOU WISH THE LEAGUE STANDINGS FOR THE SEASON TO DATE'
   @ 8,15 SAY 'ENTER '+STR(max_wk,2)+ ;
          ', THE LAST WEEK FOR WHICH DATA WERE ENTERED'
   @ 9,15 SAY 'OTHERWISE, ENTER THE WEEK DESIRED.'
   @ 11,15 GET in_wk
   READ
   IF VAL(in_wk) > max_wk .OR. VAL(in_wk) < 1
     @ 15,10 SAY 'THE WEEK INPUT IS INVALID!!!!'
     DO b:delay
     STORE '  ' TO in_wk
     CLEAR
   ELSE
     CLEAR
     EXIT
   ENDIF
ENDDO
*
*Calculate team standings for weeks 1 thru in_wk.
*
STORE 0 TO G1A,G2A,G3A,G1B,G2B,G3B
STORE 1 TO ln,wk
```

Figure 9.23   (a) First third of program module teamstd.prg.

```
DO WHILE wk <= VAL(in_wk)
  SELECT sched
  JOIN WITH bowler TO b:names FOR week=wk .AND. lane=ln .AND.;
    tnumb=bowler->tnumb FIELDS bowler->bname, tnumb. stavg
  SELECT 6
  USE b:names
  SELECT t_stats
  SEEK names->tnumb
  SELECT names
  DO WHILE .NOT. EOF()
    SELECT scores
    LOCATE FOR bname=names->bname .AND. week=wk
    IF wk=1
      IF names->stavg < 200
        STORE INT((200-names->stavg)*0.75) TO hndkp
      ELSE
        STORE 0 TO hndkp
      ENDIF
    ELSE
      STORE bname TO ha_name
      STORE wk-1 TO ha_week
      DO b:hndkp_avg
    ENDIF
    IF ln=1 .OR. ln=3 .OR. ln=5
      STORE game1+hndkp+G1A TO G1A
      STORE game2+hndkp+G2A TO G2A
      STORE game3+hndkp+G3A TO G3A
    ELSE
      STORE game1+hndkp+G1B TO G1B
      STORE game2+hndkp+G2B TO G2B
      STORE game3+hndkp+G3B TO G3B
    ENDIF
    SELECT t_stats
    REPLACE totpins WITH ;
      totpins+scores->game1+scores->game2+scores->game3
    SELECT names
    SKIP
  ENDDO
*
  IF ln=2 .OR. ln=4 .OR. ln=6
    GOTO TOP
    STORE tnumb TO teamb
    SELECT t_stats
    STORE 1 TO count
    DO WHILE count < 4
      STORE "G" + STR(count,1) + "A" TO gamea
      STORE "G" + STR(count,1) + "B" TO gameb
      IF &gamea < &gameb
        REPLACE wins WITH wins+1 FOR tnumb=teamb
        REPLACE losses WITH + losses+1 FOR tnumb=teama
      ELSE
        IF &gamea > &gameb
          REPLACE wins WITH wins+1 FOR tnumb=teama
          REPLACE losses WITH losses + 1 FOR tnumb=teamb
        ELSE
          REPLACE wins WITH wins + 0.5, losses WITH ;
            losses + 0.5 FOR tnumb=teama .OR. tnumb=teamb
        ENDIF
      ENDIF
      STORE count + 1 TO count
    ENDDO
```

Figure 9.23   (b) Second third of program module teamstd.prg.

```
*
    IF G1A + G2A + G3A < G1B + G2B + G3B
       REPLACE wins WITH wins + 1 FOR  tnumb=teamb
       REPLACE losses WITH losses + 1 FOR tnumb=teama
    ELSE
       IF G1A + G2A + G3A > G1B + G2B + G3B
          REPLACE wins WITH wins + 1 FOR tnumb=teama
          REPLACE losses WITH losses + 1 FOR tnumb=teamb
       ELSE
          REPLACE wins WITH wins + 0.5, losses WITH ;
             losses + 0.5 FOR tnumb=teama .OR. tnumb=teamb
       ENDIF
    ENDIF
    STORE 0 TO G1A,G2A,G3A,G1B,G2B,G3B
    ELSE
       GOTO TOP
       STORE tnumb TO teama
    ENDIF
    IF ln = 6
       STORE 1 TO ln
       STORE wk + 1 TO wk
    ELSE
       STORE ln + 1 TO ln
    ENDIF
    SELECT names
    USE
    ERASE b:names.dbf
ENDDO
SELECT t_stats
JOIN WITH team TO b:stats FOR tnumb=team->tnumb ;
    FIELDS wins,losses,tname,totpins
SELECT 7
USE b:stats
@ 5,10 SAY '         MONDAY NIGHT IRREGULARS BOWLING LEAGUE'
@ 6,10 SAY '         TEAM STANDINGS AT THE END OF WEEK NUMBER ' + in_wk
@ 7,10 SAY '   ===================================================='
@ 9,10  SAY ' TEAM NAME          WINS            LOSSES          TOTAL PINS'
@ 10,10 SAY ' ----------         ----            ------          -----------'
*
DO WHILE .NOT. EOF()
    @ ROW()+1,10 SAY tname  +' '+STR(wins,4,1)+ '          '+ ;
       STR(losses,4,1)+'          '+ STR(totpins,5)
    SKIP
ENDDO
SELECT stats
USE
ERASE b:stats.dbf
SELECT t_stats
REPLACE ALL wins WITH 0, losses WITH 0, totpins WITH 0
*
@ 22,10 SAY ' '
WAIT
RETURN

B>
```

Figure 9.23   (c) Last third of program module teamstd.prg.

Figure 9.24 gives the structure for the three temporary relations that are unpopulated (empty) except during the execution of eosrpt.prg. Figure 9.25 gives the structure of T_STATS, and the contents of T_STATS that will be present at both the beginning and end of execution of teampns.prg.

```
. use highgam
. list structure
Structure for database : B:highgam.dbf
Number of data records :        0
Date of last update     : 11/03/86
Field  Field name   Type         Width      Dec
    1  BNAME         Character      15
** Total **                        16
```

(a)

```
. use highser
. list structure
Structure for database : B:highser.dbf
Number of data records :        0
Date of last update     : 11/03/86
Field  Field name   Type         Width      Dec
    1  BNAME         Character      15
** Total **                        16
```

(b)

```
. use highavg
. list structure
Structure for database : B:highavg.dbf
Number of data records :        0
Date of last update     : 11/03/86
Field  Field name   Type         Width      Dec
    1  BNAME         Character      15
** Total **                        16
```

(c)

Figure 9.24   Structure of the three temporary relations that are initially unpopulated.

```
. use t_stats
. list structure
Structure for database : B:t_stats.dbf
Number of data records :        6
Date of last update     : 11/03/86
Field  Field name   Type         Width      Dec
    1  TNUMB         Numeric        1
    2  WINS          Numeric        4         1
    3  LOSSES        Numeric        4         1
    4  TOTPINS       Numeric        5
** Total **                        15
```

(a)

```
. list off
TNUMB WINS LOSSES TOTPINS
    1  0.0    0.0        0
    2  0.0    0.0        0
    3  0.0    0.0        0
    4  0.0    0.0        0
    5  0.0    0.0        0
    6  0.0    0.0        0
```

(b)

Figure 9.25   (a) Structure and (b) initial contents of the temporary relation T_STATS.

```
***********************************************************************
*Procedure name is "fileout.prg".
*Written by Glenn A. Jackson
*Oakland University, Rochester, MI 48063
*
*This procedure outputs names from several temporary relations
* created by eosrpt.prg.
*
*Procedure is called by eosrpt.prg
*
*The name of the relation to be output is contained in variable
* fname.  The relation has only one attribute: bname.
*
USE &fname
GOTO TOP
DO WHILE .NOT. EOF()
   @ROW()+1,30 SAY bname
   SKIP
ENDDO
ZAP
RETURN
```

Figure 9.26   Program module fileout.prg that is called by eosrpt.prg.

A listing of fileout.prg, the program module that outputs the contents of the relations HIGHGAM, HIGHAVG, and HIGHSER, is given in Figure 9.26.

9.10 NEED FOR AN INPUT MENU

The menu of items given in Figure 9.1 deals with getting data out of the database. The menu does nothing to help the secretary add new tuples to the database. A typical problem facing the secretary would be to add the game scores for all bowlers for week five. As was noted earlier in this chapter, the current data in the database were entered using standard dBASE III APPEND and EDIT commands. These commands have some inherent problems from a database integrity point of view; in particular, the APPEND and EDIT commands do not check for the existence of duplicate primary keys. The original database design was predicated on the fact that duplicate primary keys would not be allowed. If this condition is to be enforced, user-written software must be designed that will identify tuples being entered into the database that would cause duplicate primary keys to exist. The software would not allow these particular tuples to be stored in the database.

Figure 9.27 outlines one method of keeping duplicate primary keys from being stored in a relation. The BOWLER relation is used as an example. The attributes in BOWLER are bname, week, game1, game2, and game3, and the primary key is the composite pair of attributes ⟨bname,week⟩. Instead of using the dBASE III APPEND command to en-

```
1.  USE bowler.


2.  Input values for attributes bname, week, game1, game2,
    and game3 as variable values name, wk, g1, g2, and g3,
    respectively.

3.  COUNT the number of tuples where bname = name
    and week = wk.

4   IF COUNT = 0 then
        APPEND the new tuple to the relation
    ELSE
        output an error message and ask for
        a new tuple.
```

Figure 9.27   Logic to keep duplicate primary keys out of the BOWLER relation.

ter a new tuple directly into BOWLER, the secretary would be asked to run a program module with the logic given in Figure 9.27. This module would ask for the tuple values that the secretary wished to enter, and then COUNT the number of tuples in the relation that had the same primary key as the one trying to be entered. If the COUNT were zero, the tuple would be automatically stored in the database. If the COUNT were not zero, the tuple would not be entered. This sort of logic would have to be used for all relations in the database. A set of programs to do this is outlined as a problem at the end of the chapter.

9.11 PROBLEMS FOR CHAPTER 9

1. Determine the solutions to the following queries using a dBASE III implementation of the bowling secretary's database outlined in Figures 9.1 through 9.4. Use either a sequence of dBASE III commands, or write a short command module containing dBASE III commands, to determine the answers to the queries. Some of the solutions are rather difficult.
   a) List the names and addresses of all members of the HiRollers bowling team.
   b) Determine the total number of pins (without handicap) for team number four through week number two.
   c) Determine the total number of pins (without handicap) for the SandBaggers through week number three.
   d) How many members of the Splitters live on Robin St.?
   e) List the names of all team captains who have bowled at least one game over 160.
   f) List the names of all bowlers who have last names that begin with the letter "M."

g) List the names of all bowlers who have bowled more than one three game series with a score over 450 this season. (Avoid duplicate data in the output.)

2. The dBASE III implementation given in this chapter sends all output to the computer terminal. Modify sdbmain.prg so that the secretary is asked if a copy of all output should go to the printer.

3. The end-of-season report module (eosrpt.prg) determines the last week of the season by determining the largest week value in the SCHED relation. The program never checks the BOWLER relation to make certain that data for the last week in the season have really been entered into the database. Modify eosrpt.prg to make this check before calculating the end-of-season report.

4. Modify eosrpt.prg so that the name of the "most improved bowler" is output. This would be the bowler(s) who has the largest difference between final and starting averages.

5. The implementation has no way to account for a bowler who misses a game, or games, during one night's bowling. Modify the implementation so that when a person misses a game (resulting in a game score of zero): (a) the zero games do not affect either their season average, or their handicap; and (b) for purposes of determining team wins and losses, the zero score is replaced by the bowler's current average minus ten pins.

6. Modify bwlrst.prg so that the TOTAL PINS WITH HANDICAP is included in the output.

7. The calculation of team standings by teamstd.prg becomes very slow as the season progresses. One reason is that when teamstd.prg calls hndkp_avg.prg to calculate the current handicap, hndkp_avg.prg makes a total pins calculation that is repeated when control returns to teamstd.prg. Modify the logic so that this duplication of effort is eliminated. Program module handkp_ave.prg is given in Figure 9.28.

8. Problem 1 in Chapter 5 called for a design of the database which would store some of the "calculable attributes" (such as total pins) in the database. Implement this database and compare the execution times for the calculation of team standings against the times found with the implementation given in this chapter. Discuss some of the update problems related to the redesigned database, in comparison to the implementation given in this chapter.

9. Write a set of menu-driven program modules that will allow the secretary to append new tuples, or modify current tuples, for any relation in the database. Each module should check for duplicate primary keys, plus make any other error checks that seem reasonable and proper. (Note that when a primary key attribute is to be modified, the modify

```
********************** HNDKP_AVG.PRG ****************
*
*Module name is "hndkp_avg.prg".
*
*Written by Barbara A. MacNeil
*Modified by Glenn A. Jackson
*Oakland University, Rochester, MI 48063
*
*This module calculates the average and handicap for a given
*bowler through a given week in the season.
*The bowler's name is input in variable: bname (an attribute).
*The week is input in variable: ha_week.
*The bowler's current average is returned in variable: bavg.
*The bowler's current average is returned in variable: hndkp.
*
*This module is called by: teamstd.prg
*
ctr = 1
t_pins = 0
SELECT scores
*
*Save the current record number for scores.dbf
*
saveit = RECNO()
*
DO WHILE ctr <= ha_week
  LOCATE FOR bname=ha_name .AND. week=ctr
  t_pins = game1 + game2 + game3 + t_pins
  ctr = ctr + 1
ENDDO
*
bavg = INT(t_pins/(ha_week*3))
IF bavg < 200
  hndkp = INT((200-bavg)*0.75)
ELSE
  hndkp = 0
ENDIF
*
*Restore original record number for scores.dbf
*
GOTO saveit
*
RETURN
```

Figure 9.28   Program module hndkp_avg.prg that is called by teamstd.prg.

should be done by a deletion of the "old" tuple followed by an insertion of the "new" one.)

10. Review all program modules called by the main menu and see if any can be made to execute more rapidly by either a change in the approach, or by using better programming or database techniques. Compare the current execution time with the revised method's execution time to determine the amount of improvement in speed of response. Determine if the use of index files will have a measurable effect on execution time.[2]

---

[2]Test runs made with a hard disk system, using the same program modules given in this chapter, gave execution times that were faster by a factor of at least three.

10

IMPLEMENTING THE BOWLING SECRETARY'S DATABASE USING R:BASE 5000

This chapter contains three main sections of information and discussion: (1) sample listings of the four relations that form the bowling secretary's database as they were implemented in R:base 5000; (2) examples of how R:base 5000 commands can be used with these relations to answer simple queries; and (3) an in-depth discussion of a set of menu-driven program modules that answer complex queries using R:base 5000 commands embedded in the R:base 5000 programming language. The database implementation was developed using an IBM PC with 320K of memory, two double-sided disk drives, and a monochrome monitor. The R:base 5000 system disk is always in side A; the program modules and database files are in side B.

10.1 THE CASE STUDY DATABASE IN R:BASE 5000

Before proceeding with discussions of specific queries and various programming modules, the actual database relations will be examined. The test data in the database were developed under the same assumptions that existed in Chapter 9. The assumptions are

1. The bowling league has six teams.

2. Each team has four bowlers.

3. The season is only four weeks long.

4. Data for all four weeks have been entered using standard R:base 5000 LOAD and EDIT commands.

5. All bowlers bowl every game.

Possible changes in some of these assumptions are explored as exercises in the problems listed at the end of the chapter.

```
R>list sched

    Table: sched
    Read Password: NO
    Modify Password: NO

    Column definitions
    #  Name      Type       Length       Key
    1  tnumb     INTEGER      1 value(s)  yes
    2  week      INTEGER      1 value(s)
    3  lane      INTEGER      1 value(s)

    Current number of rows:      24

R>
```
(a)

tnumb	week	lane
1	1	1
2	1	2
3	1	4
4	1	3
5	1	6
6	1	5
1	2	4
2	2	5
3	2	2
4	2	6
5	2	1
6	2	3
1	3	3
2	3	6
3	3	1
4	3	4
5	3	5
6	3	2
1	4	5
2	4	1

tnumb	week	lane
3	4	3
4	4	2
5	4	4
6	4	6

(b)

Figure 10.1 (a) Structure and (b) contents of the SCHED relation.

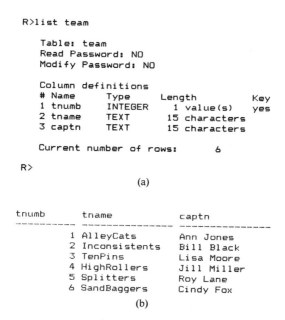

```
R>list team

    Table: team
    Read Password: NO
    Modify Password: NO

    Column definitions
    # Name       Type      Length          Key
    1 tnumb      INTEGER    1 value(s)      yes
    2 tname      TEXT      15 characters
    3 captn      TEXT      15 characters

    Current number of rows:       6

R>
```
                    (a)


```
tnumb        tname              captn
--------     --------------     ---------------
       1 AlleyCats          Ann Jones
       2 Inconsistents      Bill Black
       3 TenPins            Lisa Moore
       4 HighRollers        Jill Miller
       5 Splitters          Roy Lane
       6 SandBaggers        Cindy Fox
```
                    (b)

Figure 10.2   (a) Structure and (b) contents of the TEAM relation.

Figures 10.1 through 10.4 show both the structure and the actual test data for each relation. The data stored in these relations are the same as given in Chapter 9, so that the results of the two implementations can be compared, if one wishes to do so. The name of the database in the R:base 5000 implementation is SDB.

In looking over the data in the BOWLER relation, it is again noted (as in Chapter 9) that there appears to be a duplication of street address and phone number data. The temptation is to deduce that phone −⟩ stret is a valid FD. The reader is urged to review the reasons, given in Section 9.1, why this is not a valid FD, and why none of the stret or phone data are redundant.

10.2 ANSWERING SECRETARY QUERIES
WITH R:BASE 5000

The examples in this section are intended to illustrate the fact that simple queries concerning data in the bowling secretary's database can be made using R:base 5000 commands, without embedding those commands in a host language. All queries in this section involve the specific relations given

```
R>list bowler

Table: bowler
Read Password: NO
Modify Password: NO

Column definitions
# Name      Type      Length         Key
1 bname     TEXT      15 characters  yes
2 tnumb     INTEGER    1 value(s)
3 phone     TEXT       8 characters
4 stret     TEXT      20 characters
5 stavg     INTEGER    1 value(s)

Current number of rows:    24

R>
```
(a)

bname	tnumb	phone	stret	stavg
Jean Adams	5	689-1234	10 Robin St	111
Steve Adams	5	689-1234	10 Robin St	130
Bill Black	2	689-2345	15 Bluebird Ln	149
Bonnie Black	2	689-2345	15 Bluebird Ln	120
Bo Blow	2	689-3456	12 Meadowbrook Ln	143
Jo Blow	2	689-3456	12 Meadowbrook Ln	95
Joe Brown	3	689-4567	18 Bluebird Ln	132
Sue Brown	3	689-4567	18 Bluebird Ln	124
Cindy Fox	6	689-5678	19 Cardinal St	103
Randy Fox	6	689-5678	19 Cardinal St	147
Ann Jones	1	689-4365	12 Finch Dr	105
John Jones	1	689-4365	12 Finch Dr	143
Joy Lane	5	689-6789	21 Sparrow Ct	125
Roy Lane	5	689-6789	21 Sparrow Ct	167
Jill Miller	4	689-7890	12 Robin St	108
Paul Miller	4	689-7890	12 Robin St	170
Lisa Moore	3	689-8901	11 Lark Dr	110
Mike Moore	3	689-8901	11 Lark Dr	140
Jim Smith	1	689-9012	13 Finch Dr	152
Mary Smith	1	689-9012	13 Finch Dr	115

bname	tnumb	phone	stret	stavg
Ruth Taylor	6	689-0123	20 Cardinal St	119
Dan White	4	689-2143	16 Robin St	158
Jan White	4	689-2143	16 Robin St	121
Russel Taylor	6	689-0123	20 Cardinal St	161

(b)

Figure 10.3   (a) Structure and (b) contents of the BOWLER relation.

in Figures 10.1 through 10.4. The reader is urged to implement the database, load the relations with the test data, and check the queries that are being discussed. In many cases a sequence of two or three commands, rather than a single command, will be required to answer even relatively simple-looking queries.

The examples below assume that the user is at R:base 5000 command

```
R>list scores

     Table: scores
     Read Password: NO
     Modify Password: NO

     Column definitions
     # Name      Type      Length         Key
     1 bname     TEXT      15 characters  yes
     2 week      INTEGER    1 value(s)
     3 game1     INTEGER    1 value(s)
     4 game2     INTEGER    1 value(s)
     5 game3     INTEGER    1 value(s)

     Current number of rows:      96

  R>
```

(a)

bname	week	game1	game2	game3
Jean Adams	1	119	120	94
Steve Adams	1	112	140	138
Bill Black	1	137	155	155
Bonnie Black	1	120	125	115
Bo Blow	1	160	145	125
Jo Blow	1	101	91	93
Jim Smith	1	160	150	146
Mary Smith	1	120	110	115
Ann Jones	1	98	110	107
John Jones	1	145	150	134
Joe Brown	1	140	127	129
Sue Brown	1	121	128	124
Cindy Fox	1	119	110	83
Randy Fox	1	143	150	148
Russel Taylor	1	167	150	166
Ruth Taylor	1	110	125	122
Joy Lane	1	126	127	122
Roy Lane	1	145	180	176
Jill Miller	1	111	101	112
Paul Miller	1	180	196	134
bname	week	game1	game2	game3
Dan White	1	156	163	154
Jan White	1	130	125	108
Lisa Moore	1	99	120	111
Mike Moore	1	150	149	121

(b)

Figure 10.4   (a) Structure and (b) contents of the SCORES relation. (Only scores for week one are given. See Figure 9.4 for values for all four weeks.)

level with the R> prompt showing. It is also assumed that the bowling secretary's database has been opened with the command:

R> OPEN b:sdb

QUERY #1: "List the names of all the teams in the league."

This query is very easy to answer for two reasons: first, all the information needed to answer the query is located in one relation; and second, no qualification (WHERE clause) is required. The solution is obtained with the following command:

```
R) SELECT tname FROM team
```

or

```
R) SELECT tname +
R) FROM team
```

In the second version, the single command has been placed on two lines for readability by using the "+" character as a continuation symbol. The execution of either version will result in the listing of the names of the six teams in the league.

QUERY #2: "What is the name of the captain of team number four?"

The solution to this query is only slightly more difficult than the solution to Query #1. The increase in difficulty is due to the fact that a WHERE clause is required in the solution:

```
R) SELECT captn +
R) FROM team +
R) WHERE tnumb = 4
```

The DBMS response will be captn = Jill Miller.

QUERY #3: "Find the names of all bowlers who had a starting average less than 100."

The form of the solution to this query is very similar to that for Query #2:

```
R) SELECT bname +
R) FROM bowler +
R) WHERE stavg < 100
```

The response will be the single name: Jo Blow.

QUERY #4: "What are the names and phone numbers of all the team members of team number three?"

The solution is

> R) SELECT bname,phone +
> R) FROM bowler +
> R) WHERE tnumb = 3

The response will be

bname	phone
Joe Brown	689-4567
Sue Brown	689-4567
Lisa Moore	689-8901
Mike Moore	689-8901

QUERY #5: "On which lane does team number five bowl during the third week of the season?"

The solution to this query requires a WHERE clause with a set of conditions, rather than a single condition:

> R) SELECT lane +
> R) FROM sched +
> R) WHERE tnumb = 5 AND week = 3

The system response to this query will be lane = 5.

QUERY #6: "Find the names of all bowlers who live on Robin St."

Since addresses in the database are stored as strings of the form "21 Robin St", the solution to Query #6 requires a search, within the stret field of each tuple in the BOWLER relation, to see if the character string "Robin St" appears. The search can be accomplished through the use of the CONTAINS operator in the WHERE clause. Several solutions are possible.

> R) SELECT bname +
> R) FROM bowler +
> R) WHERE stret CONTAINS Robin St

or,

> R) SELECT bname +
> R) FROM bowler +
> R) WHERE stret CONTAINS "Robin St"

or,

R⟩ SET VAR subsrt TO Robin & St
R⟩ SELECT bname +
R⟩ FROM bowler +
R⟩ WHERE stret CONTAINS .substr

The response in all three cases will yield the same result:

bname
Jean Adams
Steve Adams
Jill Miller
Paul Miller
Dan White
Jan White

The differences among the three solutions involve the manner in which the string "Robin St" is specified. In the first two solutions, the user must make certain that exactly one space is placed between the strings "Robin" and "St", since this is the way the street addresses are stored in the database. In the last case, the "&" operator forces the system to assume only one space between the two strings it separates. One advantage of the last form is that it emphasizes the one-space condition to anyone who reviews the solution.

QUERY #7: "How many three-game series greater than 550 have been bowled to date?"

The solution to this query is complicated somewhat by the fact that R:base 5000 allows only one arithmetic operation in an expression. For example, expressions of the general form

var1 + var2

can be placed into a legal form in R:base 5000, while there is no way that an expression with two operators, like

var1 + var2 + var3

can be placed in one command. The ramification of this limitation on this particular query is that a set of temporary locations must be set up to store intermediate calculations. One way to set up the temporary locations is to add a column to the relation whose data are being analyzed. Once the final

answer has been obtained, the column is deleted from the relation. The total
solution requires a series of steps:

```
R> EXPAND scores WITH total INTEGER
R> ASSIGN total TO game1 + game2 IN scores
R> ASSIGN total TO total + game3 IN scores
R> COMPUTE number AS COUNT total +
R> FROM scores +
R> WHERE total > 550
R> SHOW VAR number
R> REMOVE COLUMN total FROM scores
```

The EXPAND command adds a new column to the SCORES relation,
names that column total, and types it as integer. The two ASSIGN commands calculate the sum (game1 + game2 + game3) for each tuple in
SCORES and places each sum in the corresponding total field. At this point
the total field in each tuple holds the sum of the three single game scores
in that tuple. The next three lines in the solution are one command: a COM-
PUTE-FROM-WHERE construct. This command counts the number of
tuples in which the total value is greater than 550 and places this count in
the variable number. This value is then printed out via the SHOW VAR
command. Finally, the column that was added to the SCORES relation is
removed with the REMOVE COLUMN command. The final answer to the
query is number = 2.

The solution proposed for Query #7 has one rather serious drawback:
the solution alters the basic structure of the SCORES relation by adding,
and then deleting, a new column. Many database practitioners do not like
to have any query alter the structure of any relation in the database, once
the database has been created. These people would argue that a temporary
relation with one or more columns (attributes) should be created to hold
the temporary data during calculations, rather than creating a new column
in one of the design relations. In this latter method, if something goes awry
during the execution of the solution, the original database would still be in
place. There is merit in this position, and the reader is urged to devise a
method for solving the last query in a manner that does not alter the basic
structure of the SCORES relation.

QUERY #8: "Who is the captain of the opponents of team number five during
          week number three?"

This query is best answered in a two-step process. First, Query #5 can
be used to determine that team number five is on lane = 5 during week
number three. This means that the opponents on that night will be bowling

on lane = 6. Using this information, the team number of the team that is bowling on lane six during the third week of the season can be found and stored in a variable, e.g. "tem":

```
R> SET VAR tem TO tnumb IN sched +
R> WHERE lane = 6 AND week = 3
```

The value stored in variable tem can now be used to determine the captain's name:

```
R> SET VAR ans TO captn IN team +
R> WHERE tnumb = .tem
R> SHOW VAR ans
```

The response will be ans = Bill Black.

QUERY #9: "List the names of all bowling league members who are not members of the SandBaggers."

This solution, like the last one, requires a mapping of information obtained from one relation into a second relation in order to obtain the correct answer. In this example the JOIN relational algebra operator will be used.

```
R> PROJECT tempr FROM team USING tnumb +
R> WHERE tname < > SandBaggers
R> RENAME COLUMN tnumb TO ttnumb IN tempr
R> JOIN tempr USING ttnumb +
R> WITH bowler USING tnumb +
R> FORMING result
R> SELECT bname +
R> FROM result
R> REMOVE result
R> REMOVE tempr
```

The output here will be a list of twenty names.

The last solution proceeds as follows: (1) A new relation called TEMPR is projected out of the TEAM relation. TEMPR has only one column, tnumb. TEMPR holds the team numbers of all teams except the SandBaggers. (2) The only column in TEMPR is renamed to ttnumb, so that it will be different from the team number column in the BOWLER relation. During the JOIN operation that is to follow, R:base 5000 expects that columns being JOINed will have different names. (3) TEMPR and BOWLER are JOINed to form a third relation, RESULT. The bname column in RESULT holds the desired names of league members. (4) The SE-LECT command displays the solution to the query. (5) The two temporary relations, RESULT and TEMPR, are removed from the database.

QUERY #10: "How many total pins (without handicap) does Bill Black have at the end of week three?"

One solution proceeds as follows:

```
R> COMPUTE tot AS SUM game1 FROM scores +
R> WHERE week < = 3 AND bname = "Bill Black"
R> COMPUTE s2 AS SUM game2 FROM scores +
R> WHERE week < = 3 AND bname = "Bill Black"
R> COMPUTE s3 AS SUM game3 FROM scores +
R> WHERE week < = 3 AND bname = "Bill Black"
R> SET VAR tot TO .tot + .s2
R> SET VAR tot TO .tot + .s3
R> SHOW VAR tot
```

The final output here is tot $= 1381$.

In this solution, the first COMPUTE command adds up all of the game1 scores for the first three weeks of the season that belong to Bill Black, and stores the sum in the variable tot. The next two COMPUTE commands repeat this process for game2 and game3, storing the respective sums in variables s2 and s3. The SET VAR commands add the values of these three variables together to obtain the final result. The SHOW VAR command outputs the final answer.

QUERY #11: "How many different bowling league members have bowled at least one game over 150?"

One solution to this query is

```
R> PROJECT tempr FROM scores USING bname +
R> WHERE game1 > 150 OR game2 > 150 OR game3 >150
R> DELETE DUPLICATES FROM tempr
R> COMPUTE ans AS ROWS FROM tempr
R> SHOW VAR ans
R> REMOVE tempr
```

The final answer is ans $= 11$.

In this solution, a temporary relation, TEMPR, is PROJECTed out of the scores relation. TEMPR has only one column, bname. There is one tuple in this relation for every tuple in the SCORES relation in which at least one single game score over 150 is present. Since the same person may have bowled games over 150 on different nights, it is possible that the same name may occur several times in TEMPR. The DELETE DUPLICATES command removes all duplicate names (tuples) from TEMPR. The remaining names are then counted via the COMPUTE command to give the final answer.

The fact that duplicate tuples are allowed in TEMPR is an indication that the R:base 5000's PROJECT is not a true relational algebra operator, and that TEMPR is not, originally, a true relation. As was stated in earlier chapters, no microcomputer-based relational database management system is fully relational, and the user must take this fact into account when making queries. R:base 5000 is closer to being a fully relational DBMS than most microcomputer-based database management systems.

In the query solutions given above, it should be noted that the solutions given are not unique. There are normally many ways in which the solution to a query can be obtained. Some solutions may execute considerably faster than others, and some may have logic that is much easier to follow. The best way to learn how to write good solutions is to study solutions written by others, and then write many solutions on your own, using several different approaches to each problem.

10.3 THE MAIN MENU FOR PREPROGRAMMED QUERY SOLUTIONS

The queries in Section 10.2 are ones that would be asked by a typical bowling secretary and, for the most part, the solutions to the queries were straightforward and not too long in terms of the number of R:base 5000 statements that it took to obtain an answer. It is assumed that the bowling secretary would enter these solutions manually, although the length of some of the solutions might easily result in errors being made in their entry. In addition, the bowling secretary would have to be fairly knowledgeable in both database theory, and the syntax of R:base 5000, in order to generate the solutions, without simply copying them from a sheet of solutions. In order to relieve the secretary of the burden of regenerating a query solution each time the same query is encountered, a menu of often-used queries can be stored, and a preprogrammed solution for each query executed every time a given query is chosen. The following sections of this chapter outline in detail one particular menu and the programs that are related to that menu.

The menu, as seen by the secretary, is given in Figure 10.5. The program module that generates the menu, accepts menu choices, and then transfers control to other program modules, is given in Figure 10.6: this is

```
┌══════ MONDAY NIGHT IRREGULARS BOWLING LEAGUE QUERY MENU ══════┐
│    (1)   DISPLAY STATISTICS FOR AN INDIVIDUAL BOWLER          │
│    (2)   DISPLAY TOTAL PINS FOR EACH TEAM                     │
│    (3)   DISPLAY TEAM STANDINGS                               │
│    (4)   DISPLAY SCHEDULE FOR A GIVEN WEEK                    │
│    (5)   GENERATE AN END-OF-SEASON REPORT                     │
│    (6)   RETURN TO RBASE 5000                                 │
└──────────────────────────────────────────────────────────────┘
```

Figure 10.5   The main menu generated by secdb.apx.

```
$COMMAND
SECDB
SET MESSAGE OFF
OPEN SDB
SET ERROR MESSAGE OFF
SET VAR PICK1   INT
LABEL STARTAPP
   NEWPAGE
   CHOOSE PICK1   FROM sdbmain   IN SECDB.APX
   IF PICK1  EQ            1 THEN
      RUN bwlrst.com
      GOTO STARTAPP
   ENDIF
   IF PICK1  EQ            2 THEN
      RUN teampns   IN SECDB.APX
      GOTO STARTAPP
   ENDIF
   IF PICK1  EQ            3 THEN
      RUN teamstd.com
      GOTO STARTAPP
   ENDIF
   IF PICK1  EQ            4 THEN
      RUN wkschdl   IN SECDB.APX
      GOTO STARTAPP
   ENDIF
   IF PICK1  EQ            5 THEN
      RUN eosrpt.com
      GOTO STARTAPP
   ENDIF
   IF PICK1  EQ            6 THEN
      GOTO ENDAPP
   ENDIF
   GOTO STARTAPP
LABEL ENDAPP
CLEAR PICK1
RETURN
$MENU
sdbmain
COLUMN   MONDAY NIGHT IRREGULARS BOWLING LEAGUE QUERY MENU
DISPLAY STATISTICS FOR AN INDIVIDUAL BOWLER
DISPLAY TOTAL PINS FOR EACH TEAM
DISPLAY TEAM STANDINGS
DISPLAY SCHEDULE FOR A GIVEN WEEK
GENERATE AN END-OF-SEASON REPORT
RETURN TO RBASE 5000
```

Figure 10.6   The main menu program module secdb.app.

named secdb.app. Secdb.app was developed using APPLICATION EX-PRESS, a software utility package that is part of the R:base 5000 package of software. To increase the speed of execution, secdb.app was compiled into an executable module with the name secdb.apx. Once R:base 5000 is brought to command level, the menu program is executed by entering the following sequence of commands:

```
R> B:
R> RUN secdb IN secdb.apx
```

When any of the first five menu choices are chosen, a program module written in R:base 5000's programming language is executed. Some of these modules call other submodules in turn. All of the program modules that are called in response to a menu choice are discussed in detail in the following sections of this chapter. The program implementations that were used to generate the outputs given in this chapter were compiled versions of the source programs whose listings will be shown.

10.4 R:BASE 5000 PROGRAM MODULE BWLRST.PRG

This module is called by the main menu program when the menu choice is "DISPLAY STATISTICS FOR AN INDIVIDUAL BOWLER." The execution of this module results in the calculation and output of several statistics for an individual bowler. The statistics can be obtained for any week in the bowling season, up to and including the last week for which scores have been entered into the database. The logic contained in this module is given in Figure 10.7, the program itself is found in Figure 10.8, and a typical output from the module is given in Figure 10.9 (p. 158).

The only portion of bwlrst.prg logic that needs to be emphasized is the handicap calculation section that consists of the two fairly harmless looking statements:

```
SET VAR hndkp TO 200 - .bavg
SET VAR hndkp TO .hndkp × 0.75
```

"hndkp" is a variable that has been declared as INTEGER, and is to hold the current handicap for a given individual. "bavg," also an INTEGER variable, holds the bowler's current average. These two statements solve the equation

$$\text{handicap} = TRUNC((\,200 - \text{current\_average})*0.75)$$

1. Determine the last week for which scores have been
    entered into the SCORES relation. Store the week
    as "max_wk."

2. Input the week of the season for which statistics
    are desired as "wk," and check the value for
    validity.

3. Input the name of the bowler for which statistics are
    desired as "name," and check the name for validity.

4. Using the SET POINTER feature of R:base 5000, identify
    all tuples in the SCORES relation that will be used
    in the calculations. (The condition is that
    bname = name AND week <= wk.)

5. For each tuple in the group selected via SET POINTER:

    a) Check each individual game score to find the
        highest game bowled by this bowler as "hi_game."

    b) Check the sum of each three game series to find
        the highest series score as "hi_series."

    c) Add all the individual game scores to find the
        total number of scratch pins as "tot_pins."

6. Calculate this bowler's current average and handi-
    cap as "bavg" and "hndkp," respectively.

7. Output the results.

Figure 10.7   General logic in bwlrst.prg.

where TRUNC is the truncation function. Although hndkp is an integer variable, the multiplication of hndkp by 0.75 results in a real value. This real value is then assigned to the integer variable hndkp. R:base 5000 automatically truncates, rather than rounds, a real number that is assigned to a variable that has been declared as INTEGER. If the real value were rounded to get the handicap, the statistics of both individuals and teams would be greatly affected.

10.5 R:BASE 5000 PROGRAM MODULE TEAMPNS.PRG

This module is called when the main menu choice is "DISPLAY TOTAL PINS FOR EACH TEAM." The total number of pins calculated is "scratch" pins, namely the pin count without considering handicaps. The modification of this module to include total pin count with handicaps is included as a problem assignment at the end of the chapter. The module is developed under the assumption that the pin count was desired through the last week for which game scores have been entered into the database. A

```
*(Procedure name is: "bwlrst.prg"                                      )
*(Written by Glenn A. Jackson                                          )
*(Oakland University, Rochester, MI 48063                              )
*(                                                                     )
*(This procedure calculates and outputs the following                 )
*( statistics on an individual bowler:  High game, High series,)
*( Total Pins and Handicap.  All statistics include all games  )
*( bowled to date.                                                     )
*(                                                                     )
*(This procedure is called by: sdbmain menu.                          )
*(This procedure calls no other modules.                              )
*(                                                                     )
NEWPAGE
SET VAR hi_game INTEGER
SET VAR hi_ser INTEGER
SET VAR bavg INTEGER
SET VAR hndkp INTEGER
SET VAR max_wk INTEGER
SET VAR wk INTEGER
SET VAR temp INTEGER
SET VAR totpins INTEGER
SET VAR name TEXT
SET VAR done TEXT
SET VAR check INTEGER
SET VAR tot3 INTEGER
SET VAR totgam INTEGER
*()
*( Find the last week for which scores were entered as max_wk )
*()
COMPUTE max_wk AS MAX week FROM scores
*()
*( Input the week for which statistics are desired as wk )
*()
SET VAR done TO "false"
WHILE done EXISTS THEN
    WRITE "IF YOU WISH THE STATISTICS FOR THE SEASON TO DATE" AT 7 15
    WRITE "ENTER " AT 8 15
    SHOW VAR max_wk=1 AT 8 21
    WRITE ", THE LAST WEEK FOR WHICH DATA WERE ENTERED" AT 8 23
    FILLIN wk USING "OTHERWISE, ENTER THE WEEK DESIRED: " AT 9 15
    IF wk GE 1 AND wk LE .max_wk THEN
       BREAK
    ENDIF
    WRITE "THE WEEK INPUT IS INVALID" AT 15 15
    WRITE "Press any key to continue.." AT 17 15; PAUSE
    NEWPAGE
ENDWHILE
*()
*( Enter the bowler's name and make certain it is valid.)
*()
NEWPAGE
WHILE done EXISTS THEN
    FILLIN name USING "ENTER THE BOWLER'S NAME, e.g. Joe Jones: " AT 10 15
    COMPUTE check AS COUNT bname FROM bowler WHERE bname = .name
    IF check GT 0 THEN
```

Figure 10.8   (a) First part of program module bwlrst.prg.

```
      BREAK
    ENDIF
    WRITE "THE NAME ENTERED IS NOT IN THE DATABASE" AT 12 15
    WRITE "Press any key ... then enter another name." AT 14 15; PAUSE
    NEWPAGE
ENDWHILE
NEWPAGE
*()
*( Calculate this bowler's statistics )
*()
SET VAR hi_game TO 0
SET VAR hi_ser TO 0
SET VAR totpins TO 0
SET POINTER #1 err1 FOR scores WHERE bname EQ .name AND week LE .wk
WHILE err1 EQ 0 THEN
    SET VAR temp TO game1 IN #1
    IF temp GT .hi_game THEN
      SET VAR hi_game TO .temp
    ENDIF
    SET VAR tot3 TO .temp
    SET VAR temp TO game2 IN #1
    IF temp GT .hi_game THEN
      SET VAR hi_game TO .temp
    ENDIF
    SET VAR tot3 TO .temp + .tot3
    SET VAR temp TO game3 IN #1
    IF temp GT .hi_game THEN
      SET VAR hi_game TO .temp
    ENDIF
    SET VAR tot3 TO .temp + .tot3
    IF tot3 GT .hi_ser THEN
      SET VAR hi_ser TO .tot3
    ENDIF
    SET VAR totpins TO .totpins + .tot3
    NEXT #1 err1
ENDWHILE
*()
*( Calculate this bowler's handicap  )
*()
SET VAR totgam TO .wk x 3
SET VAR bavg TO .totpins / .totgam
IF bavg LT 200 THEN
  SET VAR hndkp TO 200 - .bavg
  SET VAR hndkp TO .hndkp x 0.75
ELSE
  SET VAR hndkp TO 0
ENDIF
*()
*( Output the results )
*()
WRITE "STATISTICS FOR" AT 7 20
SHOW VAR name=15 AT 7 36
WRITE "THRU WEEK " AT 7 51
SHOW VAR wk=1 AT 7 61
WRITE "+++++++++++++++++++++++++++++++++++++++++++++" AT 8 20
```

Figure 10.8   (b) Second part of program module bwlrst.prg.

```
WRITE "AVERAGE PINS PER GAME: " AT 10 20
SHOW VAR bavg=3 AT 10 43
WRITE "TOTAL PINS - WITHOUT HANDICAP: " AT 12 20
SHOW VAR totpins=4 AT 12 50
WRITE "HIGH GAME SCORE TO DATE: " AT 14 20
SHOW VAR hi_game=3 AT 14 45
WRITE "HIGH SERIES TO DATE: " AT 16 20
SHOW VAR hi_ser=3 AT 16 41
WRITE "CURRENT HANDICAP: " AT 18 20
SHOW VAR hndkp=2 AT 18 38
WRITE "Press any key to continue .. " AT 23 20; PAUSE
CLEAR ALL VAR
RETURN
```

Figure 10.8 (c) Last part of program module bwlrst.prg.

```
STATISTICS FOR  Bill Black     THRU WEEK 3
++++++++++++++++++++++++++++++++++++++++++++++

AVERAGE PINS PER GAME: 153

TOTAL PINS - WITHOUT HANDICAP:1381

HIGH GAME SCORE TO DATE: 165

HIGH SERIES TO DATE: 483

CURRENT HANDICAP: 35
```

Figure 10.9 Typical output from bwlrst.prg.

sample output from the execution of this program module is given in Figure 10.10. The general logic contained in the module is found in Figure 10.11, and the source code for the module is given in Figure 10.12.

If the logic in the R:base 5000 version of teampns.prg is compared to the dBASE III version of the same module (Section 9.4), it will be found that the dBASE III version used a JOIN operation to gather together all the scores of all the bowlers from one team into a common unit of information. This information was stored in a temporary relation named TEMP2. Although a JOIN could have been used in the same manner in the

```
TOTAL SCRATCH PINS THROUGH WEEK  4
++++++++++++++++++++++++++++++++++++++
TEAM NO.   TEAM NAME      TOTAL PINS
--------   ---------      ----------
   1       AlleyCats        6257
   2       Inconsistents    6172
   3       TenPins          6147
   4       HighRollers      6798
   5       Splitters        6580
   6       SandBaggers      6534
```

Figure 10.10 Typical output from the execution of teampns.prg.

1. Determine the last week for which scores have been
    entered into the SCORES relation. Save the week
    value as "max_wk."

2. Print out the header for the table of data that will
    be output later.

3. Use an outer WHILE - THEN loop, with the variable "ctr"
    as a loop variable, to cycle through each of the six
    teams in the league. For each team, use SET POINTER #1
    to locate all the bowlers on that team:

    a) Use an inner WHILE - THEN loop to find the total
        number of pins for one team. Save the total
        as "totpins."

    b) Check the TEAM relation to find the name of the
        team for this team number. Save the team name
        as "name_t."

    c) Output the data on this team, adjusting the line
        count on the output accordingly.

Figure 10.11   General logic of teampns.prg.

R:base 5000 version, it was decided that it would be simpler from a programming point of view to use the SET POINTER operator in R:base 5000 to identify all the members on one team, and then sum all the game scores for this team using a WHILE − THEN loop. No attempt was made to determine if the SET POINTER version was faster or slower than the JOIN version in the R:base 5000 implementation.

10.6 R:BASE 5000 PROGRAM MODULE WKSCHDL.PRG

This program module is called by the main menu program when the menu choice is "DISPLAY SCHEDULE FOR A GIVEN WEEK." The execution of this module results in the output of a table giving the team names, and the lanes to which each team has been assigned for a given week in the bowling season. The module requests the week for which the schedule is desired, and verifies that the week value is valid, before proceeding with the calculations. A typical output from the execution of the module is given in Figure 10.13. The general logic contained in the module is found in Figure 10.14, and the module itself is given in Figure 10.15 (p. 162).

The heart of the logic in wkschdl.prg is implemented with a SET POINTER command followed by a WHILE − THEN construct to replace a possible JOIN operation. The use of a JOIN in this algorithm is explored as a problem at the end of this chapter.

```
*(Procedure name is "teampns"                               )
*(Written by Glenn A. Jackson                               )
*(Oakland University, Rochester, MI 48063                   )
*(                                                          )
*(This procedure prints out the total number of "scratch"   )
*(  pins for each team for the season to date.              )
*(                                                          )
*(This procedure is called by: sdbmain menu                )
*(This procedure calls:                                     )
*(                                                          )
*(No parameters are passed into or out of this module.     )
NEWPAGE
SET VAR max_wk INTEGER
COMPUTE max_wk AS MAX week FROM scores
*(Print out the header for the output data                  )
WRITE "TOTAL SCRATCH PINS THROUGH WEEK "  AT 5 20
SHOW VAR max_wk=1 AT 5 53
WRITE "+++++++++++++++++++++++++++++++++++++++++" AT 6 20
WRITE "TEAM NO.   TEAM NAME      TOTAL PINS" AT 7 20
WRITE "--------   ----------     -----------" AT 8 20
*(                                                          )
*(Calculate and print out the total pins for each team.     )
*(                                                          )
SET VAR ctr INTEGER
SET VAR lyne INTEGER
SET VAR gsum1 INTEGER
SET VAR gsum2 INTEGER
SET VAR gsum3 INTEGER
SET VAR name_t TEXT
SET VAR name_b TEXT
SET VAR totpins INTEGER
SET VAR err1 INTEGER
SET VAR ctr TO 1
*()
*(       Outer loop picks the team                          )
*()
WHILE ctr LE 6 THEN
  SET POINTER #1 err1 FOR bowler WHERE tnumb EQ .ctr
*()
*(       Inner loop picks the bowlers on a team             )
*()
  SET VAR totpins TO 0
  WHILE err1 EQ 0 THEN
    SET VAR name_b TO bname IN #1
    COMPUTE gsum1 AS SUM game1 FROM scores WHERE bname = .name_b
    COMPUTE gsum2 AS SUM game2 FROM scores WHERE bname = .name_b
    COMPUTE gsum3 AS SUM game3 FROM scores WHERE bname = .name_b
    SET VAR totpins TO .totpins + .gsum1
    SET VAR totpins TO .totpins + .gsum2
    SET VAR totpins TO .totpins + .gsum3
    NEXT #1 err1
  ENDWHILE
*( )
  SET VAR name_t TO tname IN team WHERE tnumb = .ctr
  SET VAR lyne TO .ctr + 8
  SHOW VAR ctr=1 AT .lyne 23
  SHOW VAR name_t=15 AT .lyne 30
  SHOW VAR totpins=5 AT .lyne 49
  SET VAR ctr TO .ctr + 1
ENDWHILE
WRITE "Press any key to continue..." AT 20 20; PAUSE
CLEAR ALL VAR
RETURN
```

Figure 10.12   Program module teampns.prg.

```
THE  SCHEDULE  FOR  WEEK  NUMBER  3
+++++++++++++++++++++++++++++++++++
TEAM                    LANE  NUMBER
----                    -----------
AlleyCats                    3
Inconsistents                6
TenPins                      1
HighRollers                  4
Splitters                    5
SandBaggers                  2
```

Figure 10.13   Typical output from program module wkschdl.prg.

1.   Determine the last week of the bowling season. Assign
     this value to variable "max_wk".

2.   Input the week of the season for which the schedule is
     desired as "in_val", and check to make certain that the
     value is valid.

3.   Output the header for the table of values that is to
     follow.

4.   Use a SET POINTER command in the SCHED relation to
     identify all of the tuples that have week values equal
     to the value in in_val.

5.   Use a WHILE – THEN loop to cycle through all of the
     teams that are in the set of teams linked together via
     the SET POINTER command in 4. Output the team name
     (tname) found in the TEAM relation, and the lane
     number (lane) found in the SCHED relation for each
     team.

Figure 10.14   General logic for program module wkschdl.prg.

```
$COMMAND
wkschdl
*(Procedure name is "wkschdl"                                          )
*(Written by Glenn A. Jackson                                          )
*(Oakland University, Rochester, MI 48063                              )
*(                                                                     )
*(This procedure prints out the schedule for a given week.            )
*(The week for which the schedule is desired is input from            )
*( the terminal.                                                       )
*(                                                                     )
*(This procedure is called by: sdbmain menu.                          )
*(This procedure calls: delay                                         )
*(                                                                     )
NEWPAGE
*(Find the last week of the season as max_wk                          )
SET VAR max_wk INTEGER
COMPUTE max_wk AS MAX week FROM sched
*(Input desired week value and check it for validity.                 )
SET VAR done TEXT
SET VAR done TO "false"
SET VAR in_val INTEGER
WHILE done EXISTS THEN
    WRITE "ENTER WEEK FOR WHICH SCHEDULE IS DESIRED" AT 7 10
    WRITE "ONLY VALUES BETWEEN 1 AND " AT 8 10
    SHOW VAR max_wk=1 AT 8 36
    FILLIN in_val USING " ALLOWED" AT 8 38
    IF in_val LE .max_wk AND in_val GE 1 THEN
      BREAK
    ENDIF
    WRITE "THE WEEK INPUT IS INVALID" AT 15 10
    WRITE "Press any key to continue" AT 16 10; PAUSE
    NEWPAGE
ENDWHILE
*(                                                                     )
*(Output header                                                       )
NEWPAGE
WRITE "        THE SCHEDULE FOR WEEK NUMBER " AT 5 10
SHOW VAR in_val=1 AT 5 46
WRITE "        ++++++++++++++++++++++++++++++" AT 6 10
WRITE "        TEAM                 LANE NUMBER" AT 7 10
WRITE "        ----                 -----------" AT 8 10
*(Determine and output the schedule                                   )
SET POINTER #1 err1 FOR sched WHERE week EQ .in_val
SET VAR ln INTEGER
SET VAR lyne INTEGER
SET VAR lyne TO 9
WHILE err1 EQ 0 THEN
    SET VAR numb TO tnumb IN #1
    SET VAR name TO tname IN team WHERE tnumb EQ .numb
    SET VAR ln TO lane IN #1
    SHOW VAR name=15 AT .lyne 17
    SHOW VAR ln=1 AT .lyne 41
    SET VAR lyne TO .lyne + 1
    NEXT #1 err1
ENDWHILE
WRITE "Press and key to continue.." AT 20 17; PAUSE
CLEAR ALL VAR
RETURN
```

Figure 10.15   Program module wkschdl.prg.

10.7 R:BASE 5000 PROGRAM MODULE EOSRPT.PRG

This module is called by the main menu when the menu choice is "GEN-ERATE AN END-OF-SEASON REPORT." The execution of this module results in the determination and output of the names of the bowlers who (1) had the highest single game score for the season, (2) had the highest three-game series score for the season, and (3) ended the season with the highest per game average.

The output from this module for the data in the sample database is given in Figure 10.16. The general logic for the module is found in Figure 10.17, and the module itself is given in Figure 10.18.

10.8 R:BASE 5000 PROGRAM MODULE TEAMSTD.PRG

This program module is called by the main menu program when the menu choice is "DISPLAY TEAM STANDINGS." The execution of teamstd.prg results in the calculation and display of the won–lost record for all teams in the league through a given week in the season. The total number of "scratch" pins for each team through that week in the season is also output. The module begins by requesting the week for which the standings are desired. After making certain that the week entered is valid, the program proceeds to calculate the standings and print out the results in tabular form. Figure 10.19 shows a typical output from the execution of the program. Figure 10.20 gives the general logic for the module, and the source code is given in Figure 10.21. See pages 167–72.

```
                    END-OF-SEASON REPORT
                    ++++++++++++++++++++

            HIGHEST SINGLE GAME SCORE OF 202
            WAS BOWLED BY THE FOLLOWING BOWLER(S)
                        Roy Lane
                        Russel Taylor
                        Paul Miller


            HIGHEST THREE-GAME SERIES SCORE OF 559
            WAS BOWLED BY THE FOLLOWING BOWLER(S)
                        Roy Lane
                        Paul Miller


            HIGHEST AVERAGE GAME SCORE OF 179
            WAS BOWLED BY THE FOLLOWING BOWLER(S)
                        Paul Miller
```

Figure 10.16   Output of eosrpt.prg for the sample database.

1. Determine the last week of the season from the SCHED relation. Save this value as "max_wk."

2. Determine the highest single game score for the season. Save this score as "best_gam."

3. Output the high game score information:

   a) PROJECT a unary temporary relation TEMPR from SCORES that holds the names (bname) of all bowlers who have bowled at least one game score equal to the value in best_gam.
   b) Print out the end-of-season report header followed by the names of all those people who bowled the highest single game score.
   c) REMOVE the temporary relation TEMPR from the database.

4. Determine the highest three-game series score as "best_ser" as follows:

   a) EXPAND the SCORES relation with the addition of a new column named total.
   b) Fill the total field value in each tuple with the sum game1+game2+game3 from that tuple.
   c) Find the best_ser value using the COMPUTE - MAX command on the total field in SCORES.
   d) PROJECT a temporary relation TEMPR from SCORES that holds the names of all bowlers with a three-game score of best_ser.
   e) Output the information on best series.

5. Determine the season's best average game score as "best_avg" as follows:

   a) PROJECT a temporary relation, TEMP2, from the BOWLER relation that holds each bowler's name (bname) and starting average (stavg).
   b) Change the column name stavg to avg in TEMP2.
   c) Calculate the average game score for each bowler and fill in the avg field value in TEMP2 with this value.
   d) Compute the value for best_avg using a COMPUTE-MAX command and output the final results.
   e) Output the information on best average.

6. REMOVE COLUMN total from SCORES.

7. REMOVE TEMP2 from the database.

Figure 10.17   General logic for eosrpt.prg.

```
*(Procedure name is "eosrpt.prg"    )
*(Written by Glenn A. Jackson  )
*(Oakland University, Rochester, MI   48063)
*()
*(This procedure calculates and prints out the end-of-season report)
*()
*(This procedure is called by: sdbmain menu)
*(This procedure calls no other modules    )
*()
NEWPAGE
SET MESSAGE OFF
SET ERROR MESSAGE OFF
*()
*(Find the last week of the season as max_wk)
*()
SET VAR max_wk INTEGER
COMPUTE max_wk AS MAX week FROM sched
*(Initialize variables required for the report)
SET VAR best_ser INTEGER
SET VAR best_avg INTEGER
SET VAR best_gam INTEGER
SET VAR name TEXT
SET VAR hg1 INTEGER
SET VAR hg2 INTEGER
SET VAR hg3 INTEGER
SET VAR linect INTEGER
*()
*(Find season's high game score as best_gam )
*()
COMPUTE hg1 AS MAX game1 FROM scores
COMPUTE hg2 AS MAX game2 FROM scores
COMPUTE hg3 AS MAX game3 FROM scores
IF hg1 >= .hg2 THEN
  SET VAR best_gam TO .hg1
ELSE
  SET VAR best_gam TO .hg2
ENDIF
IF hg3 > .best_gam THEN
  SET VAR best_gam TO .best_gam + .hg3
ENDIF
*()
*(Place the names of all those who got best_gam in TEMPR)
*()
PROJECT tempr FROM scores USING bname +
WHERE game1 = .best_gam OR game2 = .best_gam OR game3 = .best_gam
DELETE DUPLICATES FROM tempr
*()
*(Print out the end-of-season report header and high game data)
*()
WRITE "END-OF-SEASON REPORT" AT 1 26
WRITE "+++++++++++++++++++++" AT 2 26
WRITE "HIGHEST SINGLE GAME SCORE OF " AT 4 20
SHOW VAR best_gam=3 AT 4 49
WRITE "WAS BOWLED BY THE FOLLOWING BOWLER(S)" AT 5 20
SET VAR linect TO 6
```

Figure 10.18   (a) First part of program module eosrpt.prg.

```
SET POINTER #1 err1 FOR tempr
WHILE err1 = 0 THEN
  SET VAR name TO bname IN #1
  SHOW VAR name=15 AT .linect 30
  SET VAR linect TO .linect + 1
  NEXT #1 err1
ENDWHILE
REMOVE tempr
*()
*(Find the season's high three-game series score as best_ser)
*( and output the results)
*()
EXPAND scores WITH total INTEGER
ASSIGN total TO game1 + game2 IN scores
ASSIGN total TO total + game3 IN scores
COMPUTE best_ser AS MAX total FROM scores
PROJECT tempr FROM scores USING bname +
WHERE total = .best_ser
DELETE DUPLICATES FROM tempr
SET VAR linect TO .linect + 2
WRITE "HIGHEST THREE-GAME SERIES SCORE OF" AT .linect 20
SHOW VAR best_ser=3 AT .linect   55
SET VAR linect TO .linect + 1
WRITE "WAS BOWLED BY THE FOLLOWING BOWLER(S):" AT .linect 20
SET VAR linect TO .linect + 1
SET POINTER #1 err1 FOR tempr
WHILE err1 = 0 THEN
  SET VAR name TO bname IN #1
  SHOW VAR name=15 AT .linect 30
  SET VAR linect TO .linect + 1
  NEXT #1 err1
ENDWHILE
REMOVE tempr
*()
*(Find the highest season's average as best_avg)
*( and output the results)
*()
SET VAR tgames INTEGER
SET VAR totpins INTEGER
SET VAR tgames INTEGER
SET VAR err1 INTEGER
SET VAR err2 INTEGER
PROJECT temp2 FROM bowler USING bname stavg
CHANGE COLUMN stavg IN temp2 TO avg
SET VAR tgames TO .max_wk x 3
SET POINTER #1 err1 FOR temp2
WHILE err1 = 0 THEN
  SET VAR name TO bname IN #1
  COMPUTE totpins AS SUM total FROM scores +
  WHERE bname = .name
  ASSIGN avg TO .totpins / .tgames IN temp2 WHERE bname = .name
  NEXT #1 err1
ENDWHILE
COMPUTE best_avg AS MAX avg FROM temp2
*()
```

Figure 10.18   (b) Second part of program module eosrpt.prg.

```
SET VAR linect TO .linect + 2
WRITE "HIGHEST AVERAGE GAME SCORE OF " AT .linect 20
SHOW VAR best_avg=3 AT .linect 50
SET VAR linect TO .linect + 1
WRITE "WAS BOWLED BY THE FOLLOWING BOWLER(S)" AT .linect 20
SET VAR linect TO .linect + 1
SET POINTER #2 err2 FOR temp2 +
WHERE avg = .best_avg
WHILE err2 = 0 THEN
  SET VAR name TO bname IN #2
  SHOW VAR name=15 AT .linect 30
  SET VAR linect TO .linect + 1
  NEXT #2 err2
ENDWHILE
REMOVE temp2
REMOVE COLUMN total FROM scores
SET MESSAGE ON
SET ERROR MESSAGE ON
WRITE "Press any key to continue.." AT 21 20; PAUSE
RETURN
```

Figure 10.18   (c) Last part of program module eosrpt.prg.

```
        MONDAY NIGHT IRREGULARS BOWLING LEAGUE
           STANDINGS AT THE END OF WEEK 1

    tnumb       wins        losses      totpins
   ---------   ---------   ---------   ---------
        1       2.00000     2.00000       1545
        2       2.00000     2.00000       1522
        3       1.00000     3.00000       1519
        4       3.00000     1.00000       1670
        5       2.50000     1.50000       1599
        6       1.50000     2.50000       1593
```

Figure 10.19   Typical output from program module teamstd.prg.

The logic in teamstd.prg is more complex than any of the other modules in the implementation. Because of a design decision made in Chapter 5, the number of wins, losses, and total pins for each team at the end of each week are not stored in the database. This was done to avoid the possibility of having inconsistent data in the database in those cases where someone might alter a league member's game score without recalculating the effect that this change would have on wins, losses, and total pins. One result of this design decision is that, when team standings are calculated for any week, the standings must be recalculated for every week preceding the week in question, starting with week one. This not only complicates the logic in teamstd.prg, but drastically increases the time that is required to calculate the results. The calculation time for the generation of team standings increases fairly linearly with the number of weeks into the season for which the standings are desired. Namely, it takes about three times as long to calculate the standings for week three as it does for week one.

1. Determine the last week of the season for which scores
    have been entered into the SCORES relation. Save this
    value as "max_wk."

2. Input the week for which the standings are desired as
    "in_wk," and make certain that value input is valid.

3. Zero the wins, losses, and totpins values in all tuples
    in the extra relation TSTATS.

4. For each lane (noted as ln), do the following for
    each week (noted as wk):

    a) Use the SET POINTER #2, WHILE-THEN combination to
        operate on the scores for each bowler on the team
        bowling on this lane for this week. The following
        things are done for each bowler: (1) their current
        handicap is calculated and stored in "hndkp"; (2)
        each individual game score is added to the team
        total for that game for that night (including
        handicap); (3) the totpins value in TSTATS for this
        team is replaced with the current value plus the
        sum of this bowler's three game total (without
        handicap).

        The coding used here is that g1a is the total pin
        count for game1 for the team on the odd numbered
        lane, while g1b is the total pin count for game1 for
        the team on the even numbered lane. g2a, g3a, g2b,
        and g3b have similar meanings.

    b) Adjust the won-lost record (in TSTATS) of the last
        two teams analyzed. The coding here is that the
        team on the odd numbered lane has its identifier
        names ending with "a," while the team on the even
        numbered lane has identifiers that end in "b."

5. Output the league standings by merely SELECTing all the
    data that are in TSTATS, after a proper heading has been
    output.

Figure 10.20   General logic for teamstd.prg.

Since wins, losses, and total pins are not stored as part of the basic
set of relations in the database, a temporary relation was developed to hold
these data only during the time that calculations are being made in the generation of team standings. The relation is

TSTATS(tnumb,wins,losses,totpins)

and the contents of TSTATS that are present when the calculation of team
standings begins is shown in Figure 10.22 (p. 173). To make certain that

```
*(Procedure name is "teamstd.prg" )
*(Written by Glenn A. Jackson      )
*(Oakland University, Rochester, MI 48063)
*()
*(This procedure calculates and prints out the league standings )
*( for any week.  The week desired is input from the terminal.  )
*()
*(Procdure is called by sdbmain menu )
*()
NEWPAGE
SET VAR max_wk INTEGER
SET VAR in_wk INTEGER
SET VAR done TEXT
*(Determine the last week for which scores have been entered as max_wk )
COMPUTE max_wk AS MAX week FROM scores
*()
*(Enter week for which the standings are desired .. and verify )
*()
SET VAR done TO "false"
WHILE done EXISTS THEN
    WRITE "ENTER WEEK FOR WHICH LEAGUE STANDINGS ARE DESIRED" AT 7 10
    WRITE "ONLY VALUES BETWEEN 1 AND " AT 8 10
    SHOW VAR max_wk=1 AT 8 36
    FILLIN in_wk USING " ALLOWED " AT 8 38
    IF in_wk LE .max_wk AND in_wk GE 1 THEN
      BREAK
    ENDIF
    WRITE "THE WEEK INPUT IS INVALID" AT 15 10
    WRITE "Press and key to continue" AT 16 10; PAUSE
    NEWPAGE
ENDWHILE
*()
SET VAR err1 INTEGER
SET VAR err2 INTEGER
SET VAR err3 INTEGER
SET VAR tot   INTEGER
SET VAR avg   INTEGER
SET VAR tnb   INTEGER
SET VAR hndkp INTEGER
SET VAR teama INTEGER
SET VAR teamb INTEGER
SET VAR tota INTEGER
SET VAR totb INTEGER
SET VAR name TEXT
SET VAR g1a TO 0
SET VAR g2a TO 0
SET VAR g3a TO 0
SET VAR g1b TO 0
SET VAR g2b TO 0
SET VAR g3b TO 0
SET VAR ln  TO 1
SET VAR wk  TO 1
*()
*( Make certain than wins, losses and totpins attribute values )
*( are all zero in the scratch-pad relation TSTATS, before new )
```

Figure 10.21   (a) First part of program module teamstd.prg.

```
*( team standing calculations begin.)
*()
ASSIGN wins TO 0.0 + 0.0 IN tstats
ASSIGN losses TO 0.0 + 0.0 IN tstats
ASSIGN totpins TO 0 + 0 IN tstats
*()
*(Calculation of standings begins here -  calculations go a week)
*(at-a-time from wk = 1 to in_wk.)
*()
WHILE wk <= .in_wk THEN
     SET POINTER #1 err1 FOR sched WHERE week = .wk AND lane = .ln
     SET VAR tnb TO tnumb IN #1
     SET POINTER #2 err2 FOR bowler WHERE tnumb = .tnb
     WHILE err2 = 0 THEN
       SET VAR name TO bname IN #2
*()
     IF wk = 1 THEN
       SET VAR avg TO stavg IN #2
     ELSE
       RUN getavg.prg  *(FIND THE avg TO USE FOR THIS WEEK)
     ENDIF
     IF avg < 200 THEN
         SET VAR hndkp TO 200 - .avg
         SET VAR hndkp TO .hndkp x 0.75
     ELSE
         SET VAR hndkp TO 0
     ENDIF
*()
     SET POINTER #3 FOR scores WHERE bname = .name AND week = .wk
     SET VAR g1 TO game1 IN #3
     SET VAR g2 TO game2 IN #3
     SET VAR g3 TO game3 IN #3
     IF ln = 1 OR ln = 3 OR ln = 5 THEN
       SET VAR g1a TO .g1a + .g1
       SET VAR g1a TO .g1a + .hndkp
       SET VAR g2a TO .g2a + .g2
       SET VAR g2a TO .g2a + .hndkp
       SET VAR g3a TO .g3a + .g3
       SET VAR g3a TO .g3a + .hndkp
     ELSE
       SET VAR g1b TO .g1b + .g1
       SET VAR g1b TO .g1b + .hndkp
       SET VAR g2b TO .g2b + .g2
       SET VAR g2b TO .g2b + .hndkp
       SET VAR g3b TO .g3b + .g3
       SET VAR g3b TO .g3b + .hndkp
     ENDIF
     SET VAR tot TO .g1 + .g2
     SET VAR tot TO .tot + .g3
     ASSIGN totpins TO totpins + .tot IN tstats WHERE tnumb = .tnb
     NEXT #2 err2
   ENDWHILE
*()
*(When an even numbered lane is present, calculate wins and losses)
*( for the team on this lane and the team on the odd numbered lane)
```

Figure 10.21   (b) Second part of program module teamstd.prg.

```
*( before it.)
*()
   IF ln = 2 OR ln = 4 OR ln = 6 THEN
     SET VAR teamb TO .tnb
     IF g1a > .g1b THEN
        ASSIGN wins TO wins + 1.0 IN tstats WHERE tnumb = .teama
        ASSIGN losses TO losses + 1.0 IN tstats WHERE tnumb = .teamb
     ELSE
        IF g1b > .g1a THEN
           ASSIGN wins TO wins + 1.0 IN tstats WHERE tnumb = .teamb
           ASSIGN losses TO losses + 1.0 IN tstats WHERE tnumb = .teama
        ELSE
           ASSIGN wins TO wins + 0.5 IN tstats +
             WHERE tnumb = .teama OR tnumb = .teamb
           ASSIGN losses TO losses + 0.5 IN tstats +
             WHERE tnumb = .teama OR tnumb = .teamb
        ENDIF
     ENDIF
*()
     IF g2a > .g2b THEN
        ASSIGN wins TO wins + 1.0 IN tstats WHERE tnumb = .teama
        ASSIGN losses TO losses + 1.0 IN tstats WHERE tnumb = .teamb
     ELSE
        IF g2b > .g2a THEN
           ASSIGN wins TO wins + 1.0 IN tstats WHERE tnumb = .teamb
           ASSIGN losses TO losses + 1.0 IN tstats WHERE tnumb = .teama
        ELSE
           ASSIGN wins TO wins + 0.5 IN tstats +
             WHERE tnumb = .teama OR tnumb = .teamb
           ASSIGN losses TO losses + 0.5 IN tstats +
             WHERE tnumb = .teama OR tnumb = .teamb
        ENDIF
     ENDIF
*()
     IF g3a > .g3b THEN
        ASSIGN wins TO wins + 1.0 IN tstats WHERE tnumb = .teama
        ASSIGN losses TO losses + 1.0 IN tstats WHERE tnumb = .teamb
     ELSE
        IF g3b > .g3a THEN
           ASSIGN wins TO wins + 1.0 IN tstats WHERE tnumb = .teamb
           ASSIGN losses TO losses + 1.0 IN tstats WHERE tnumb = .teama
        ELSE
           ASSIGN wins TO wins + 0.5 IN tstats +
             WHERE tnumb = .teama OR tnumb = .teamb
           ASSIGN losses TO losses + 0.5 IN tstats +
             WHERE tnumb = .teama OR tnumb = .teamb
        ENDIF
     ENDIF
*()
     SET VAR tota TO .g1a + .g2a
     SET VAR tota TO .tota + .g3a
     SET VAR totb TO .g1b + .g2b
     SET VAR totb TO .totb + .g3b
     IF tota > .totb THEN
        ASSIGN wins TO wins + 1.0 IN tstats WHERE tnumb = .teama
```

Figure 10.21   (c) Third part of program module teamstd.prg.

```
        ASSIGN losses TO losses + 1.0 IN tstats WHERE tnumb = .teamb
    ELSE
      IF totb > .tota THEN
         ASSIGN wins TO wins + 1.0 IN tstats WHERE tnumb = .teamb
         ASSIGN losses TO losses + 1.0 IN tstats WHERE tnumb = .teama
      ELSE
         ASSIGN wins TO wins + 0.5 IN tstats +
            WHERE tnumb = .teama OR tnumb = .teamb
         ASSIGN losses TO losses + 0.5 IN tstats +
            WHERE tnumb = .teama OR tnumb = .teamb
      ENDIF
    ENDIF
*()
    SET VAR g1a TO 0
    SET VAR g2a TO 0
    SET VAR g3a TO 0
    SET VAR g1b TO 0
    SET VAR g2b TO 0
    SET VAR g3b TO 0
  ELSE
    SET VAR teama TO .tnb
  ENDIF
  IF ln = 6 THEN
    SET VAR ln TO   1
    SET VAR wk TO .wk + 1
  ELSE
    SET VAR ln TO .ln + 1
  ENDIF
ENDWHILE
*()
*(Output the league standings for the week value input above.)
*()
NEWPAGE
WRITE "    MONDAY NIGHT IRREGULARS BOWLING LEAGUE" AT 5 1
WRITE "        STANDINGS AT THE END OF WEEK " AT 6 1
SHOW VAR in_wk=1 AT 6 36
WRITE " "
SELECT ALL FROM tstats
WRITE  "Press and key to continue.." AT 22 5; PAUSE
RETURN
```

Figure 10.21   (d) Last part of program module teamstd.prg.

this relation holds no data from previous calculations, the values of wins, losses, and totpins are all set to zero at the start of execution of teamstd.prg. (One way to speed up the execution of this module would be to save the data in this relation from week to week. However, this would be a programming method of circumventing the design decision that kept these values out of the database in the first place.

The main point of confusion, which may be encountered by the reader in looking over the logic in teamstd.prg, is the way in which teams on adjacent lanes get paired together. The logic first determines the tnumb of the team that is assigned to lane one for a given week by using SET POINTER #1 on the SCHED relation (see Figure 10.23). The tnumb obtained via pointer #1 is used to locate all the members of that team using SET POINTER #2 on the BOWLER relation. The individual game scores for

```
R>list tstats

     Table: tstats
     Read Password: NO
     Modify Password: NO

     Column definitions
     # Name      Type       Length         Key
     1 tnumb     INTEGER      1 value(s)
     2 wins      REAL         1 value(s)
     3 losses    REAL         1 value(s)
     4 totpins   INTEGER      1 value(s)

     Current number of rows:        6

  R>
```

(a)

```
R>select all from tstats
   tnumb        wins        losses       totpins
  ----------  -----------  -----------   ---------
           1    0.00000      0.00000
           2    0.00000      0.00000
           3    0.00000      0.00000
           4    0.00000      0.00000
           5    0.00000      0.00000
           6    0.00000      0.00000
  R>
```

(b)

Figure 10.22   (a) The structure of TSTATS, and (b) the contents of TSTATS at the start of execution of teamstd.prg.

the bowler found using pointer #2, for the team from pointer #1, is obtained using SET POINTER #3 on the SCORES relation.

The game scores of all team members bowling on lane one are stored in variables that end in an "a," such as g1a. The "a" implies the team on the odd numbered alley, for the two teams being considered. When the lane variable (ln) is switched to lane two, the scores of all the team members from this team are stored in variables that end in "b," such as g1b. The "b" implies the team on the even numbered alley, for the two teams being considered. Once all the scores of all the members of two teams have been analyzed, the wins and losses for that week can be determined. At this point the same procedure is used on the teams assigned to the next two lanes. This process continues until all the teams have been analyzed.

The relation TSTATS must be created before teamstd.prg can be used. Although the relation is left in the database from run to run, it is not a regular relation since its contents are assumed to be incorrect at the start of each execution of teamstd.prg. It is a temporary relation in the sense that its data are created, output, and then destroyed. The values found in this relation are not intended to be used from run to run. Some database

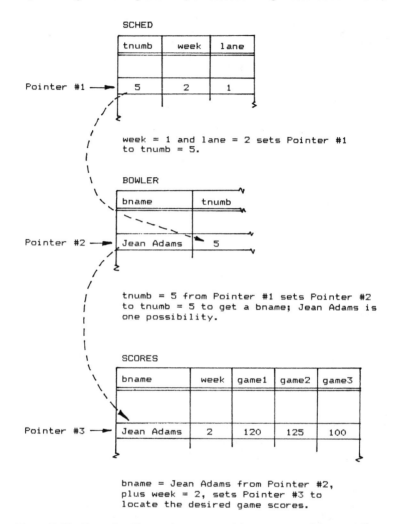

Figure 10.23 Example of how pointers are used in program module teamstd.prg.

management systems have commands for creating the structure of temporary relations during the execution of a program. These temporary relations exist, and can be used like any other relation, as long as the program that created them is active. When the creating program terminates execution, the temporary relations disappear.

Teamstd.prg calls one procedure: getavg.prg. This module, listed in Figure 10.24, calculates the average that is required for the handicap calculation for a given week, for a given bowler. For instance, if teamstd.prg is calculating the wins and losses that were earned during week four of the

```
*(Procedure name is "getavg.prg"  )
*(Written by Glenn A. Jackson      )
*(Oakland University, Rochester, MI 48063)
*()
*(This procedure calculates the average to be used to calculate )
*( the handicap for a given bowler for a given week in the season.)
*( The week is input via the global variable "wk"; the bowler's)
*( name is input via the global variable "name", and the average)
*( is output via the global variable "avg".  Input and output)
*( variables are defined as integers in the calling program .)
*( This module is called only when the week input is greater)
*( than one.)
*()
*(Procedure is called by teamstd.prg )
*()
SET VAR sum     INTEGER
SET VAR s1      INTEGER
SET VAR s2      INTEGER
SET VAR s3      INTEGER
SET VAR numgams INTEGER
*()
COMPUTE s1 AS SUM game1 FROM scores +
   WHERE bname = .name AND week < .wk
COMPUTE s2 AS SUM game2 FROM scores +
   WHERE bname = .name AND week < .wk
COMPUTE s3 AS SUM game3 FROM scores +
   WHERE bname = .name AND week < .wk
SET VAR sum TO .s1 + .s2
SET VAR sum TO .sum + .s3
SET VAR numgams TO .wk - 1
SET VAR numgams TO .numgams x 3
SET VAR avg TO .sum / .numgams
RETURN
```

Figure 10.24   Program module getavg.prg.

season, the handicap used in these calculations uses the average on the first three weeks of the season. Getavg.prg calculates this average for each bowler.

10.9 PROBLEMS WITH INPUTTING NEW DATA INTO THE DATABASE

The menu of items given in Figure 10.5 deals with getting data out of the database. The menu does nothing to help the secretary add new tuples to any relation in the database. As was noted earlier in this chapter, the data that are currently in the database were entered using standard R:base 5000 LOAD and EDIT commands. It would be helpful to the bowling league secretary if an input menu were developed that would guide the secretary through the entry of commonly encountered additions, such as entering all of the bowler's scores for a new week in the season. This problem is left as an exercise at the end of the chapter.

To help protect the integrity of the data in the database, R:base 5000 has incorporated a RULES command. This command is used to define conditions that force the DBMS to check on certain restrictions that the user sets on the data in the database. Once a rule is defined for a specific relation, the system checks every modification of data and every addition of data to the relation. For instance, if the user wishes to make certain that there is at most one tuple in the TEAM relation with a given team number (tnumb is the primary key), then the following rule must be placed on the TEAM relation via the RULES command:

"Duplicate Key" tnumb IN team NEA tnumb IN team

"Duplicate Key" is the error message that will be printed out each time an attempt is made to violate this condition, and NEA stands for 'not equal to any'. Problem 10 at the end of the chapter deals with conditions of this type.

10.10 COMMENTS ON CHAPTER 10

As long as a query involves only the retrieval of information from a database, the query solution can probably be solved using R:base 5000 commands at command level. Some of these solutions may involve a series of commands that require a fairly good understanding of database philosophy. These solutions cannot be developed by someone who is untrained in the field.

If a query involves both retrieval and manipulation of data from the database, the solution normally will require that the database commands be embedded in a host language. These solutions can become fairly involved, and must be developed by someone who is familiar with database philosophy, and who has a reasonable level of programming skill.

10.11 PROBLEMS FOR CHAPTER 10

1. The R:base 5000 menu implementation given in this chapter sends all output to the computer terminal. Add an option to the menu that will allow the secretary to choose the output devices to be used for the current run. Reasonable choices would be terminal only, printer only, and both printer and terminal.

2. Expand the menu given in Figure 10.5 through the addition of new program modules that will answer some of the longer query solutions given in Section 10.2.

3. Repeat Problem 1 from Chapter 9 using the R:base 5000 implementation.

4. Repeat Problem 3 from Chapter 9 using the R:base 5000 implementation.

5. Modify teamstd.prg so that the final standings are output in a more professional looking format. In the current implementation the standings are output using a SELECT ALL command.

6. Modify bwlrst.prg so that the TOTAL PINS WITH HANDICAP is included in the output.

7. The teampns.prg currently outputs the total number of "scratch pins" for each team. Modify the program so that the "TOTAL PINS WITH HANDICAP" is also output.

8. The main portion of the logic in the wkschdl.prg module is implemented using a SET POINTER followed by a WHILE − THEN construct. Rewrite this section using a JOIN and determine whether there is any noticeable change in the speed of execution of the module. Which of the two solutions is easier to follow?

9. Repeat Problem 9 in Chapter 9 using the R:base 5000 implementation.

10. Use the RULES command to set restrictions on each relation such that the primary keys of each relation will be unique.

11. Write a set of menu driven program modules that will allow a bowling league secretary, who is not too knowledgeable about databases, to add to the database the game scores for all teams for any week in the season. The module should give the secretary a reasonable set of prompts, and a template for the entry of the proper data. Have the module make any reasonable checks on the data being entered that aren't already being checked via the RULES set up in Problem 10.

12. Review the modules that are currently slow in execution, such as teamstd.prg, and investigate various methods of reducing execution time. (A good class contest is to see who can generate the program module that executes the fastest.)

13. Repeat Problem 5 in Chapter 9 using the R:base 5000 implementation.

II

REFLECTIONS
AND FURTHER
CONSIDERATIONS

This text was not written with the intention of having it be a compendium of all there is to know about relational database design and implementation. In keeping with this philosophy, a great deal of material that is part of the body of knowledge called relational databases was not discussed at all. This chapter will be used as a place to reflect on what has been presented, and to point out a few of the many areas of database technology that were omitted.

11.1 OTHER NORMAL FORMS

The design methods based on FD's that were discussed in Chapters 3, 4, and 5 are well documented in the literature. They have been used in a wide variety of applications and have proven to be effective design tools. As one might have suspected, no single design tool will provide the best design for all of the database problems that a designer might encounter. Situations will arise in which the data that are to be stored in a database, are related in such a manner that special design techniques must be applied to obtain the best design. As an example, there are normal forms, more restrictive than BCNF, which have been developed to avoid undesirable characteristics that can be present even in BCNF relations. Two of these forms, 4NF and DK/NF, are discussed in most advanced texts on database design. 4NF deals with relations in which sets of repeated data exist, and decomposition using FD's does not eliminate the redundancy. Decomposition into 4NF requires the use of **multi-valued dependencies** (MVD's), a concept which was felt to be beyond the intent of this text. DK/NF (domain-key normal form) can be thought of as the ultimate normal form, in the sense that no modification anomalies can occur in DK/NF relations. As yet, no formal design techniques have been developed to help a designer move a relation into this normal form.

Although they were not discussed, there are two normal forms that are less restrictive than BCNF. These forms, known as 2NF and 3NF, are valuable from a historical perspective. 2NF was developed to eliminate anomalies that could occur in 1NF relations, 3NF was developed to eliminate anomalies that could occur in 2NF relations, and so on. Very few databases are designed with the intent of having the resulting relations be only in 2NF or 3NF. It is sufficient to note that if a relation is in BCNF, it is also in 2NF and 3NF.

A subject that is closely related to the decomposition of relations from one normal form to a higher form is non-loss decomposition. This subject was mentioned in Chapter 3 and detailed in Appendix B. The brevity of the discussion given to this topic should not be interpreted as an indication of a lack of importance. It is a subject worthy of further thought and study by the reader.

11.2 ADVANTAGES OF THE ENTITY-RELATIONSHIP METHOD

In the introduction to the ER method in Chapter 6, it was noted that the ER method has several advantages over design methods that are based on FD's:

1. The design begins with an in-depth study of the overall data storage problem. This approach gives the designer a much greater feel for the problem at hand, than is obtained by starting the design with the investigation of attributes and functional dependencies.

2. The ER design philosophy can be used effectively in problems where large numbers of attributes make FD-based design methods unmanageable.

The ER presentation given in this text should give the reader a good foundation on which to begin building the expertise required for the solution of many database design problems. The designer must remember that even when the design is based on the ER philosophy, FD's cannot be forgotten; final design relations must always be checked for normal form.

11.3 WHAT PRICE NORMALIZATION?

When the goals of database design were first discussed in Chapter 2, it was stated that a good design would result in the decomposition of one or more original relations into several normalized relations. It was noted, however, that the generation of new relations would make the answering of queries to the database more complex than if queries were answered on a database made up of fewer relations. So there is somewhat of a design dilemma: should the designer worry mainly about keeping all relations in the database in BCNF, or should the main worry be one of keeping the number of relations limited in order to simplify database usage? There is no single answer to this problem.

There is a major corporation that has developed a large database in which all of the data are stored in one relation that is not even in first normal form. The personnel in charge of the database contend that they are fully aware of the problems they can get into by not having the database designed to BCNF specifications, but their primary goals are speed of access and simplicity of query format. They contend that they know what anomalies could be generated because the database is not in BCNF but they feel that, if they are careful, the anomalies will be avoided. To ensure that this is the case, users are given only a limited set of query and update options; these are made available to them through specially designed software.

The case discussed in the last paragraph, where a database consisted of one non-1NF relation, is not a typical situation. Most database administrators insist that all databases are designed so that every relation in every database is at least in BCNF. Their considered opinion is that most users are not knowledgeable enough in database theory to avoid some of the pitfalls that are present in non-BCNF designs. These designers are willing to pay the price of increased query and update complexity to ensure that the integrity of the data in the database is protected.

Regardless of the design method being used, when the database design process appears to be reaching an end, the proposed design must be evaluated from a practical standpoint, as well as from a technical standpoint. Two points that must not be overlooked are illustrated by the following questions:

1. Will the proposed database implementation allow standard queries to be answered fast enough to be useful? How long will it take the DBMS to respond while using the proposed database?

2. Can queries be answered in a reasonable manner, as opposed to requiring professional programmers to generate query solutions? If programmers are required, does this meet the needs of the enterprise?

If the answer to any of these questions is no, the design may have to be reevaluated.

There are several ways that a designer can attempt to speed up the response of a database to queries:

1. Index those relations that are searched regularly using the same attribute as the key for the search.

2. Replace commands, such as a JOIN, that can be shown to be taking a large amount of time to execute, with more primitive, but faster, constructs.

3. If a query is being solved using a program written in a high level language, be certain that there is not a simpler, more direct, algorithm for solving the problem.

4. Review the original design philosophy to see if some earlier decisions have come back to haunt the end product. A good example of this was the decision made in the secretary's database problem in Chapter 5 to refrain from storing any attribute whose value could be calculated from other attributes in the database. Was the improvement in integrity gained by this decision worth the resulting increase in execution time?

11.4 CONCURRENT DATABASE USAGE

The programs presented in Chapters 9 and 10 were written for a DBMS in which only one user would be using the database at every instant of time. Many database management systems allow for a database to be opened by several, or possibly many, users at the same time. Under these conditions, it is the responsibility of each user to notify the DBMS of exactly what relations are to be used, and the manner in which each of those relations will be used. Additionally, each user must notify the DBMS as to which restrictions are to be placed on the use of relations for other users of the database. For instance, one user might wish to retrieve information from relation R1 and, while this retrieval is taking place, request that no other user be allowed to delete tuples, modify tuples, or store tuples in relation R1. Systems that have this capability have special commands that are used to control concurrent processing. One of the earliest relational database management systems that featured a fairly complete set of commands for the control of concurrent processing is the Multics Relational Data Store (MRDS) by Honeywell Information Systems.[1]

An application of database management systems that is unavoidably related to concurrent processing is the use of computer networks in conjunction with database management systems. In some implementations, the database does not reside solely in one location, but is distributed over several computer systems that are tied together by a communications network. Both dBASE III Plus and R:base 5000 have some networking capabilities. The reader is urged to refer to the manufacturer's reference manual for details.

11.5 DATABASE ADMINISTRATION

No attempt has been made in this text to broach the subject of database administration. Problems related to the use of passwords and the encryption of data for security reasons, or, making backup copies of the database so that recovery can be made from errors that are inflicted on the database, are very worthy of discussion, but were not within the intent of this text.

A universal technique used by database administrators to help enforce database security is the use of **views,** or **submodels.** Under this system, a given user is allowed to use only a portion of the total database. The database is, in effect, logically partitioned to restrict the access of each individual user. Most of the recently developed database management systems have this capability.

---

[1]Multics Relational Data Store Reference Manual, Order Number AW53-04A, Honeywell Informations Systems, 1983.

Appendix A

RELATIONAL ALGEBRA

Relational algebra consists of a set of high level operators that operate on relations to generate new relations. SELECT, PROJECT, and JOIN are the names given to three of the most commonly used relational algebra operators. All DBMS query languages have commands that are functionally equivalent to the SELECT, PROJECT, and JOIN, even though they may use different names for those commands. This appendix will define the three operators, show their basic operational characteristics, and give examples of how they have been implemented in both dBASE III and R:base 5000. All examples will be related to the two relations shown in Figure A.1.

Relation ABC holds the names of students, the room to which each student has been assigned, and the phone number of the phone that has been rented to the student. Relation DEF holds information on the type of phone that is associated with each phone number. Attributes Rphone and Phone are from the same domain of campus phone numbers.

A.1 THE SELECT RELATIONAL ALGEBRA OPERATOR

The SELECT relational algebra operator operates on one existing relation to generate one new relation. The new relation is obtained by SELECTing only those tuples from the original relation that meet a specified condition.

ABC

Name	Room	Rphone
Jill	234	3256
John	126	1267
Zippy	126	5298

DEF

Phone	Type
1267	Dial
3256	PshBtn
3623	Pay
4311	Dial
5298	PshBtn

Figure A.1 Sample relations ABC and DEF.

The general form of the SELECT relational operator is

```
SELECT FROM Relation_Name
WHERE Condition
GIVING Result_Name
```

In this definition, "Relation_Name" is the name of the original relation, "Condition" is the condition that is to be used to select the tuples, and "Result_Name" is the name of the relation which will hold the result of the operation.

As an example of the use of the general form of the operator, assume that a new relation is to be generated from relation DEF(Phone,Type) by selecting those tuples where the Type value is Dial. The general form of the command would be

```
SELECT FROM DEF
WHERE Type = 'Dial'
GIVING RESULT
```

The result of this operation would be the relation given in Figure A.2. In practice, RESULT is either placed in disk storage as a temporary relation, or merely output to the terminal, depending upon the DBMS being used. If the result is output to the terminal, the headings indicating the relation and attribute names may not be output with the data, again depending upon the DBMS.

To illustrate the last example in dBASE III and R:base 5000, it will be assumed that the ABC and DEF relations have been created and stored in a database named APPNDXA.

The SELECT operation can be generated in three ways in dBASE III: using the LIST command, using the DISPLAY command, or using the COPY command. LIST and DISPLAY send the results to the terminal, while COPY places the information in a newly created relation in disk storage. Examples of each of these commands are given below, with actual executions given in Figure A.3.

RESULT

Phone	Type
1267	Dial
4311	Dial

Figure A.2 The relation obtained through a SELECT operation.

```
. USE DEF
. LIST OFF FOR Type = 'Dial'
PHONE  TYPE
1267   Dial
4311   Dial
.
. DISPLAY OFF FOR Type = 'Dial'
PHONE  TYPE
1267   Dial
4311   Dial
.
. COPY TO RESULT FOR Type = 'Dial'
        2 records copied
. USE RESULT
. LIST ALL
Record#   PHONE  TYPE
      1   1267   Dial
      2   4311   Dial
```

Figure A.3 Ways to generate a SELECT in dBASE III.

```
.USE DEF
.LIST OFF FOR Type = 'Dial'
.DISPLAY OFF FOR Type = 'Dial'
.COPY TO RESULT FOR Type = 'Dial'
```

The USE DEF command activates the relation that is to be used. The OFF portion of the LIST and DISPLAY commands prevents the DBMS from outputting the record numbers of the tuples that are selected, in addition to the tuples themselves. The output of the LIST and DISPLAY commands is sent to the screen, outputting only those tuples that satisfy the WHERE condition. If the record number for each tuple is desired in the output, the word OFF is dropped from the command. An example of this is given in Figure A.3.

The COPY command creates a new file named RESULT and stores the newly generated relation in that file. If the user wishes to see the contents of RESULT, the complete relation can be SELECTed by following the COPY command with

```
.USE RESULT
.LIST ALL
```

This was done in Figure A.3.

```
R>OPEN APPNDXA
 Database exists
R>SELECT ALL +
R>FROM DEF +
R>WHERE Type EQ Dial
 Phone        Type
 ----------   ----------
         1267 Dial
         4311 Dial
R>
```

Figure A.4 Generating a SELECT in R:base 5000.

The SELECT operation in R:base 5000 has been implemented in a manner that is very similar to the general form given above. The R:base 5000 syntax required to SELECT all the tuples from DEF where the type of phone is Dial is

```
R)OPEN APPNDXA
 Database exists
R)SELECT ALL +
R)FROM DEF +
R)WHERE Type EQ Dial
```

The R⟩ symbols shown are prompts from the R:base 5000 control system: the words "Database exists" are output by R:base 5000, indicating that the database was opened. The "+" characters used in the command indicate that more of the current command is continued on the next line. An actual run with this example is given in Figure A.4. Note that the word Dial is not enclosed in single quotes in the R:base 5000 command, even though it is a character string value.

A.2 THE PROJECT RELATIONAL OPERATOR

The PROJECT relational algebra operator operates on one existing relation to generate one new relation. The new relation is obtained by picking (PROJECTing out) only certain columns from the current relation. If the result of the PROJECT operation contains duplicate tuples, only one of each set of duplicates is retained in the new relation. (Most microcomputer-based DBMS's do not automatically remove duplicate tuples, but leave this for the user to handle. It should be remembered that a legitimate relation cannot have duplicate tuples.)

The general form of the PROJECT operation is

```
PROJECT a1,a2,..,an
FROM Relation_Name
GIVING Result_Name
```

In this definition, "a1,a2,...,an" represents the list of attribute names that are the names of the columns that are to be projected out of the relation identified by "Relation_Name." The result of the operation will be stored in a relation named "Result_Name." As a specific example of the general form, assume that it is desired to PROJECT out the Name and Room columns from ABC. The general syntax to do this is

> PROJECT Name,Room
> FROM ABC
> GIVING RESULT

The resulting relation would be the one shown in Figure A.5.

To illustrate the way that duplicate tuples are removed from the result of the general PROJECT operation, assume that the Type column is projected out DEF(Phone,Type). The general syntax to perform this operation is

> PROJECT Type
> FROM DEF
> GIVING RESULT

The result of this operation would be the relation shown in Figure A.6, where duplicate tuples holding Dial and PshBtn have been removed. (A relation, such as RESULT, that has only one column is called a unary relation. Although unary relations can be generated using the PROJECT operation, unary relations are never stored in a database, since they contain a minimal amount of information.)

The PROJECT operation in dBASE III is achieved using variations of the same commands used for generating a SELECT. Three options are

RESULT

Name	Room
Jill	234
John	126
Zippy	126

Figure A.5   A projection out of relation ABC.

RESULT

Type
Dial
PshBtn
Pay

Figure A.6   A projection with duplicate tuples removed.

available, and will be illustrated by showing how to PROJECT Name and Room from ABC.

```
.USE ABC
.LIST Name,Room
.DISPLAY ALL Name,Room
.COPY TO RESULT FIELDS Name,Room
```

Examples of each of these commands on an actual database are given in Figure A.7. Note that the LIST and DISPLAY commands send the results to the terminal. (They can also be routed to the printer.) The COPY command sends the result to a relation on the disk. The record numbers in the output can be eliminated by using the word OFF with the LIST and DISPLAY commands.

The last example in Figure A.7 is the projection of Type out of DEF and illustrates the fact that dBASE III does not automatically delete duplicate tuples from relations.

The PROJECT operator in R:base 5000 can be implemented as a variation of the SELECT command. To perform the two specific projections on DEF discussed above, the commands would be

```
R)OPEN APPNDXA
R)SELECT Name Room +
R)FROM ABC
```

```
. USE ABC
. LIST Name,Room
Record#   Name    Room
      1   Jill    234
      2   John    126
      3   Zippy   126

.
. DISPLAY ALL Name,Room
Record#   Name    Room
      1   Jill    234
      2   John    126
      3   Zippy   126

.
. COPY TO RESULT FIELDS Name,Room
RESULT.dbf already exists, overwrite it? (Y/N) Yes
      3 records copied

.
. USE RESULT
. LIST ALL
Record#   NAME    ROOM
      1   Jill    234
      2   John    126
      3   Zippy   126
```

Figure A.7 Generating a PROJECT in dBASE III.

```
R>SELECT Name Room +
R>FROM ABC
 Name        Room
 --------    --------
 Jill             234
 John             126
 Zippy            126
R>
R>SELECT Type +
R>FROM DEF
 Type
 --------
 Dial
 PshBtn
 Pay
 Dial
 PshBtn
R>
```

Figure A.8 Generating a PROJECT in R:base 5000.

and

```
R)SELECT Type +
R)FROM DEF
```

The results of executing these commands on an actual database are given in Figure A.8. (Note that duplicate tuples exist again.) If the results of a projection are to be saved as a relation in the database, the actual R:base 5000 PROJECT command would have to be used.

A.3 THE JOIN RELATIONAL ALGEBRA OPERATION

The JOIN operator creates one new relation from two existing relations. The new relation is obtained by concatenating (joining together) tuples from the first relation with tuples from the second relation. The only tuples that are concatenated are those tuples where the attribute value of a specific attribute in the first tuple is equal to the attribute value of a specific attribute in the second tuple. (The two attributes must be from a common domain.) If the first relation involved in the JOIN has N columns and the second relation has M columns, the resulting relation will have M + N columns. Two of the columns in the result will always have identical values. If one of these columns is removed, the result is termed a NATURAL JOIN.

The general form of the JOIN operator is

```
JOIN Relation_1 AND Relation_2
OVER Attribute_1 and Attribute_2
GIVING Result_Name
```

"Relation_1" and "Relation_2" identify the two relations that are to participate in the JOIN. "Attribute_1" (from Relation_1) and "Attribute_2" (from Relation_2) identify the attributes that are to be used to determine which tuples will end up in the final result. (The two attributes must be from the same domain.) "Result_Name" is the name of the relation to which the output of the operation will be assigned.

As a specific example, assume that ABC and DEF are to be joined over the common domain of campus phone numbers:

```
JOIN ABC AND DEF
OVER Rphone AND Phone
GIVING RESULT
```

The result of this operation would be the relation shown in Figure A.9. Note that the values in Rphone and Phone are identical. The elimination of one of these columns (by PROJECTion) would give the NATURAL JOIN.

To perform the JOIN operation in either dBASE III or R:base 5000, the JOIN command from that query language is used. The exact syntax in each case is different. To perform the last example in dBASE III:

```
.SELECT 2
.USE DEF
.SELECT 1
.USE ABC
.JOIN WITH DEF TO RESULT FOR Rphone = DEF - >Phone
```

The result of executing this sequence of commands on an actual database is given in Figure A.10.

To perform the same operation in R:base 5000:

```
R)OPEN APPNDXA
   Database exists
R)JOIN ABC USING Rphone +
R)WITH DEF USING Phone +
R)FORMING RESULT
   Successful join operation
```

RESULT

Name	Room	Rphone	Phone	Type
Jill	234	3256	3256	PshBtn
John	126	1267	1267	Dial
Zippy	126	5298	5298	PshBtn

Figure A.9 The relation obtained through a JOIN.

```
. SELECT 2
. USE DEF
. SELECT 1
. USE ABC
. JOIN WITH DEF TO RESULT FOR Rphone = DEF->Phone
      3 records joined
. USE RESULT
. LIST OFF
NAME   ROOM RPHONE PHONE TYPE
Jill   234  3256   3256  PshBtn
John   126  1267   1267  Dial
Zippy  126  5298   5298  PshBtn
```

Figure A.10   Generating a JOIN in dBASE III.

```
R>OPEN APPNDXA
 Database exists
R>JOIN ABC USING Rphone +
R>WITH DEF USING Phone +
R>FORMING RESULT
 Successful join operation       3 rows generated
R>SELECT ALL +
R>FROM RESULT
 Name      Room        Rphone      Phone       Type
 --------- ----------- ----------- ----------- -------
 Jill      234         3256        3256 PshBtn
 John      126         1267        1267 Dial
 Zippy     126         5298        5298 PshBtn
R>
```

Figure A.11   Generating a JOIN in R:base 5000.

Here, the R:base 5000 DBMS outputs the message "Successful join operation," after the resulting relation has been placed in disk storage. To look at the results the user must execute the command:

R>SELECT ALL FROM RESULT

This sequence of commands is illustrated in Figure A.11.

A.4 COMBINING COMMANDS

Both dBASE III and R:base 5000 have query command structures that allow for combining two types of operations into one command. For instance, to both SELECT and PROJECT in one command using R:base 5000, the command would be

```
R)OPEN APPNDXA
R)SELECT Name, Rphone +
R)FROM ABC +
R)WHERE Name EQ John
```

In this command, the columns to be projected are actually specified in the SELECT portion of the command, while the selection condition is specified in the WHERE portion. The reader is urged to review the DBMS manuals supplied by the manufacturer for further examples.

Appendix *B*

NON-LOSS
DECOMPOSITION

The decomposition design algorithm discussed in Chapter 3 takes a single relation, such as R(X,Y,Z), and decomposes it by projecting out two new relations: R1(X,Y) and R2(Y,Z). One question that must be answered with respect to this procedure is: "Will a query answered using R1(X,Y) and R2(Y,Z) give exactly the same result as an equivalent query answered using the original relation?" If it doesn't, then the design algorithm will generate a set of relations that will produce inconsistent data.

Relations obtained through decomposition will always produce consistent results, if the decomposition was made in such a manner that a natural join of R1(X,Y) and R2(Y,Z) yields exactly the original R(X,Y,Z). A decomposition which has this characteristic is called a "non-loss decomposition under a natural join." If the natural join of R1 and R2 produces more tuples than were in R originally, the decomposition is said to be "lossy."

The decomposition of R(X,Y,Z) into R1(X,Y) and R2(Y,Z) is guaranteed to be non-loss if the attribute that is common to the two projections, Y in this case, has at least one of the other two attributes dependent upon it. That is, if Y $-\rangle$ X, or Y $-\rangle$ Z, the decomposition is non-loss.

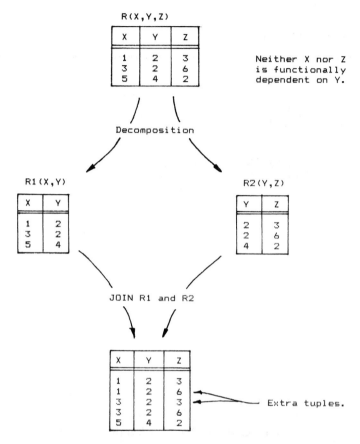

Figure B.1 Example of a lossy decomposition.

Figure B.1 is an example of a lossy decomposition. In this example, neither Y $-\rangle$ X, nor Y $-\rangle$ Z, is a valid FD, and the natural join of R1 and R2 produces two extra tuples. Figure B.2 is an example of a non-loss decomposition. In this example, X $-\rangle$ Z is assumed to be valid, and the values in the instance of R(X,Y,Z) reflect this fact. The natural join of R1 and R2 in this case produces the original relation exactly.

To illustrate the type of problem that a lossy decomposition can cause, look at the query: "What Z value is associated with an X value of 1?" Using dBASE III syntax, the query could be answered using R(X,Y,Z) with the statements:

```
.USE R
.LIST OFF Z FOR X = 1
```

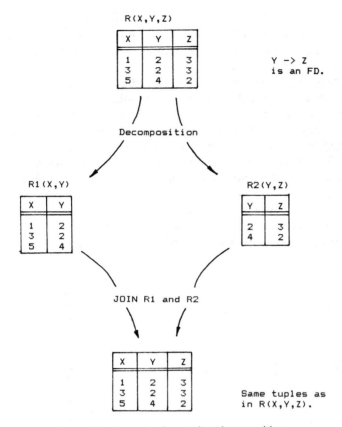

Figure B.2 Example of a non-loss decomposition.

In the instances of R given in both Figure B.1 and B.2, the answer to the query would be Z = 3. If the query is to be answered using the projections R1 and R2, the query statements should be

```
.SELECT 2
.USE R2
.SELECT 1
.USE R1
.JOIN WITH R2 TO RESULT;
   FOR X = 1 .AND. Y = R2 − ⟩Y FIELDS Z
.USE RESULT
.LIST OFF
```

Using R1 and R2 from Figure B.1 (the lossy decomposition), this solution will yield two values of Z: 3 and 6. Using R1 and R2 from Figure B.2 (the non-loss decomposition), the query will yield only the correct value: $Z = 3$. The $Z = 6$ value from the first case is inconsistent with the original data, and is a direct result of the lossy decomposition. The non-loss decomposition case gave the correct result.

The concept presented in this appendix is very simple, yet very important. The database designer must remember that if the relations in a database were generated by a lossy decomposition, some query solutions will generate extraneous data. Conversely, if the relations in a database were generated by a non-loss decomposition, query solutions will generate the same values as would have been obtained from the original relation(s). The basic decomposition algorithm given in Chapter 3 gives non-loss decompositions.

In the discussion of non-loss decomposition given above, X, Y, and Z were assumed to be single attributes. In general, X, Y, and Z can be either single attributes, or sets of attributes.

Appendix C

SUMMARY OF FILES USED WITH THE CASE STUDY DATABASES

Figure C.1 is a listing of the files used in the dBASE III implementation of the Bowling Secretary's Database given in Chapter 9. Figure C.2 is a listing of the files used in the R:base 5000 implementation given in Chapter 10.

```
Volume in drive B has no label
Directory of   B:\

SDBMAIN    PRG      1602    11-03-86     1:17p
SCHED      DBF       231     5-09-86     1:31p
WKSCHDL    PRG      1676     6-08-86     8:57p
TEAM       DBF       323     5-10-86     4:27p
DELAY      PRG       418     6-01-86    10:01p
SCORES     DBF      2691     5-20-86     4:44p
BWLRST     PRG      2871     6-10-86     2:37p
TEAMPNS    PRG      1263     6-08-86     8:41p
BOWLER     DBF      1347     5-20-86     4:05p
EOSRPT     PRG      2432    11-11-86     6:20p
HIGHSER    DBF        99    11-03-86     1:43p
HIGHGAM    DBF       115    11-03-86     1:43p
HIGHAVG    DBF        99    11-03-86     1:44p
FILEOUT    PRG       531     5-19-86     7:51p
TEAMSTD    PRG      4736    11-11-86     6:39p
T_STATS    DBF       253    11-03-86     2:00p
NUMB       NDX      1024     5-21-86     9:25a
FINDWK     PRG       804     5-22-86     2:54p
HNDKP_AV   PRG      1023     5-28-86     1:23p
        19 File(s)        328704 bytes free
```

Figure C.1 List of the files used with the database implementation given in Chapter 9.

```
Volume in drive B has no label
Directory of   B:\

SDB1       RBS      9600     2-10-87    10:20p
SDB2       RBS     10752     2-10-87    10:20p
SDB3       RBS      1024     2-10-87    10:20p
SECDB      API     12064     6-19-86     2:24p
SECDB      APX     13568     9-28-86    12:16p
EOSRPT     PRG      3840     9-28-86    11:13a
BWLRST     COM      4793     9-28-86    11:26a
BWLRST     CMD      3840     9-24-86     3:02p
SECDB      APP      5888     9-28-86    12:14p
EOSRPT     COM      5465     9-28-86    11:28a
TEAMSTD    COM      9653     9-28-86    11:32a
GETAVG     PRG      1154     9-10-86     6:56p
TEAMSTD    PRG      6528     9-12-86     1:52p
        13 File(s)        268288 bytes free

A>
```

Figure C.2 List of the files used with the database implementation given in Chapter 10.

REFERENCES

1. Chen, P. P. S. "The Entity-Relationship Model—Toward a Unified View of Data," *ACM Transactions on Database Systems*, vol. 1, no. 1 (March, 1979), pp. 9–36.

2. Date, C. J. *An Introduction to Database Systems,* vol. 1, (4th ed.). Reading, MA and Menlo Park, CA: Addison-Wesley Publishing Co., Inc., 1986.

3. Date, C. J. *An Introduction to Database Systems,* vol. 2. Reading, MA and Menlo Park, CA: Addison-Wesley Publishing Co., 1983.

4. Date, C. J. *Database: A Primer.* Reading, MA and Menlo Park, CA: Addison-Wesley Publishing Co., 1983.

5. Hawryszkiewycz, I. T. *Database Analysis and Design.* Chicago: Science Research Associates, Inc., 1984.

6. Howe, D. R. *Data Analysis for Data Base Design.* Baltimore, MD: Edward Arnold/University Park Press, 1983.

7. Kroenke, D. M., and D. E. Nilson. *Database Processing for Microcomputers.* Chicago: Science Research Associates, 1986.

8. Ullman, J. D. *Principles of Database Systems* (2nd ed.). Rockville, MD: Computer Science Press, 1982.

9. Vasta, J. A. *Understanding Data Base Management Systems.* Belmont, CA: Wadsworth Publishing Co., 1985.

INDEX

A

Anomaly, 27
  deletion, 16, 28
  insertion, 15, 27
  update, 16, 28
Attribute, 3, 12–13, 48–50, 61
  augmentation, 37
  calculable, 57
  values, 3

B

Binary relationship (See Relationship)

Bowling secretary's database, 47–57, 87
Boyce Codd Normal Form (BCNF), 23, 53–55 (*See also* Normal form)

C

Calculable attribute, 57
Candidate Key, 22–26, 53–54
  (*See also* Key)
Cardinality, 5
Conceptual model, 7–8
Concurrent database, 182